D1147160

WATER RESOURCES

Prepared for the Course Team by Sandy Smith

S268 Physical Resources and Environment

Course Team

Dave Williams (Course Chair)
Andrew Bell
Geoff Brown
Steve Drury
Chris Hawkesworth
Ian Nuttall (Editor)
Janice Robertson (Editor)
Peter Sheldon
Sandy Smith
Peter Webb
Chris Wilson
John Wright
Annemarie Hedges (Course Manager)
Charlie Bendall (Course Coordinator)

Production

Jane Sheppard (Graphic Designer)
Steve Best (Graphic Artist)
David Jackson (Series Producer, BBC)
Nicholas Watson (BBC Producer)
John Greenwood (Liaison Librarian)
Eira Parker (Course Secretary)
Marilyn Leggett (Secretary)
Lynn Tilbury (Secretary)

Course assessor

Professor Peter W. Scott, Camborne School of Mines.

Dedication

Professor Geoff Brown was a member of the Course Team when he was killed on the Galeras Volcano, Colombia, in January 1993. The Course Team dedicates S268 to his memory.

Acknowledgements

The Course Team gratefully acknowledges the contributions of members of the S238 course team (S238 *The Earth's Physical Resources*, 1984).

The Course Team also wishes to thank Sheila Dellow for careful reading of early drafts of the course material.

The Open University, Walton Hall, Milton Keynes MK7 6AA.

First published 1995. Reprinted (with corrections) 1998, 2002.

Copyright © 1995 The Open University.

Edited, designed and typeset by The Open University.

Printed in the United Kingdom by Henry Ling Limited, The Dorset Press, Dorchester, DT1 1HD

ISBN 0 7492 5147 6

This text forms part of an Open University second level course. If you would like a copy of Studying with the Open University, please write to the Central Enquiry Service, PO Box 200, The Open University, Walton Hall, Milton Keynes, MK7 6YZ. If you have not already enrolled on the course and would like to buy this or other Open University material, please write to Open University Educational Enterprises Ltd, 12 Cofferidge Close, Stony Stratford, Milton Keynes, MK11 1BY, United Kingdom.

Edition 1.3

S268block3i1.3

CONTENTS

1 WATER USE

1.1 Water as a resource

Water is the most important physical resource studied in this Course as it is the only one that is essential for human survival; we would die very quickly without it. Other physical resources can make life more comfortable, but water makes life possible. If you were shipwrecked on a desert island, your first priority would be to find a source of fresh water fairly quickly; the thought of looking for other physical resources on the island, such as gravel or ore deposits, would come much later, if at all.

Water is the commonest substance on the Earth's surface. It exists on land, in the oceans and in the atmosphere. It occurs in different physical states, as a liquid, as solid ice or snow and as gaseous water vapour in the atmosphere. Water may be pure or contain dissolved substances, particularly salt, present in waters of the oceans, some lakes and deep underground. The term 'water resources' usually refers to *fresh* water, with a low content of dissolved, suspended and biological substances, and although water is abundant on Earth, fresh water is less so, being only a few per cent of the total water, and for some parts of the Earth it is unfortunately very scarce.

Water differs from most of the other resources studied in this Course, as it is a *renewable* resource, driven in a cycle by the energy of the Sun and the Earth's gravity. For example, rain falling on land flows away to the sea in rivers, and so is temporarily lost as a fresh water resource. But rain will fall again, replenishing the rivers. The rainfall may be irregular or seasonal, so the renewability of water is not instantaneous but has a delay of a few days or even years. In comparison with the time needed to form other resources, such as sand and gravel, coal, or petroleum, this time is very short, and water is regarded as renewable.

Considerable problems are caused by the presence of too little or too much water, causing droughts or floods. The 1970s and early 1980s were a time of widespread drought in the Sahel zone of Africa, in the southern republics of the former USSR, and, on a smaller scale, parts of Britain experienced drought conditions in 1975–76 and 1988–92.

Historical water use

Early humans were hunter–gatherers, roaming from place to place, but their movements were controlled by the need for water. When humans started to grow food, establishing permanent settlements, water was needed for crops and animals as well as people, so settlements have always grown up near reliable sources of water. Most major towns lie on the banks of rivers, or, where there are no streams or rivers, settlements exist where there is water underground that can be reached by digging wells.

The management of water resources has a long history. The oldest known dam in the world was constructed in Egypt about 5000 years ago, and was used for storing drinking and irrigation water. Farmers in Arabia at this time used the craters of extinct volcanoes as storage tanks for irrigation water and

dug deep wells for their drinking water. Excavated ruins in India of similar antiquity retain the remains of water-supply and drainage systems, which included baths and swimming pools.

The Romans had sophisticated systems for water supply and sewage disposal in their cities, including great aqueducts to bring pure water from surrounding hills such as at Segovia in Spain (which was illustrated in Figure 2a of Block 2 *Building Materials*) and the Pont-du-Gard in France.

The system of using water to carry sewage disappeared with the decline of the Roman Empire, and it was only in the early nineteenth century that water closets began to be installed.

The amount of water needed for survival is very small. The desert island castaway could live on one or two litres of drinking water a day if he or she also had a source of food. However, our everyday water requirements are greater than those of the castaway. Even at subsistence level water is needed for cooking and washing as well as for drinking. The minimum requirement is about 5 litres per person per day, provided there is enough rainfall for growing food. The typical quantity of water used at subsistence level in developing countries is 20–40 litres per person per day. Here people often have no access to safe drinking water; water may be taken directly from a river, pond or well, and used without any form of treatment. However, if water is taken from a well, it is likely to be of good quality because of the purifying properties of the rock through which it has passed.

Industrialized countries, where a piped water supply is usually available, use much more water — a typical overall figure is 500 litres per person per day. Much of this extra demand comes from industry, agriculture and power generation, but part is due to the greater use of water for domestic purposes. The convenience of a piped water supply makes it easy to use water for many purposes other than drinking, cooking and basic washing — for example, washing machines, dishwashers, car washing and flushing lavatories. Indeed, in some communities, notably the drier regions of the United States, more than half the domestic water supply is used for watering lawns and flower gardens, a need that would not even be thought of by a subsistence-level community. However, on a global scale, only 8% of water use is for domestic purposes.

Table 1 gives an indication of the quantities of water needed for various domestic purposes, for growing food and for manufacturing.

Table 1 Water requirements for various domestic purposes, food growing and manufacturing

Use or product	Quantity of water needed/litres
Domestic use	
flushing lavatory, per flush	6–22
bath	80–170
shower, per minute	5–10
automatic washing-machine load	70–110
dishwasher load	55
watering garden for one hour	1000–1300
Food growing	
1 kg wheat	1000
1 kg rice	4500
1 kg sugar beet	1000
1 kg potatoes	550
Manufacturing	
1 kg (litre) beer	8
1 kg paper	15–40
1 kg bricks	1–2
1 kg steel	5–200
1 kg aluminium	1500
1 kg fertilizer	600
1 kg refined crude oil	15
1 kg synthetic rubber	3000
car (1200 kg)	30 000
car per kg	25

Note: 1 litre of water weighs 1 kg.

Question 1

You may remember seeing statements in advertisements of the kind that 'a shower uses less water than a bath'. From Table 1, is this necessarily correct?

Rainfall provides most of the water needed by crops in large areas of the world, but in some areas the rainfall is insufficient or seasonal, and vast quantities of irrigation are needed to grow crops. On a global scale, more water is used for irrigation than for anything else. Agriculture accounts for 69% of the world water use, of which most is for irrigation (see Box below).

Industry is the second largest user of water on a global scale, using 23%. Industry uses water in many ways. From Table 1 you can see that it generally needs much more than a litre (a kilogram) of water to make a kilogram of product. In addition to the purposes listed in Table 1, water is used in the preparation of processed food (such as food-canning), for cleaning, in ore-processing, for waste disposal and for cooling. Electricity generation uses vast quantities of water for cooling, as well as smaller amounts in boilers, where it is converted to steam which drives the turbines that generate electricity. In addition, the energy of falling water, usually released from a reservoir, is used to turn turbines to generate hydroelectric power.

Water is used in the production of energy, but energy is also needed to produce water: from the human energy needed to carry water from a river or raise it from a well, to the electrical energy needed to pump water around the distribution system to houses and industry. Also part of the energy budget for water resources is the energy used in building dams, digging tunnels, building water treatment plants and so on. Given enough energy, water resources can even be 'created': seawater, for example, can be desalinated to fresh water for an energy cost of about 300 megajoules per cubic metre ($300\,MJ\,m^{-3}$). (A joule, J, is the SI unit of energy, and will be used extensively in Block 4 *Energy*; $1\,MJ$ is $10^6\,J$.)

Irrigation

Irrigation is used to grow crops in areas where they could otherwise not be grown, or to improve the yield. Around 15% of the world's arable land is irrigated. In arid regions, farming would be impossible without it, as in the deserts of Egypt and Saudi Arabia. Elsewhere, irrigation is used to supplement rainfall and to overcome the high variability of rainfall in semi-arid regions, where rainfall occurs for only a short period during the year and in unpredictable quantities. Irrigation provides security against crop failure and is not confined to arid and semi-arid areas; it is used often, but irregularly, on high-value crops in areas of greater rainfall such as England.

Irrigation is most common in Asia, where it is used particularly for rice-growing in flooded fields. In some parts, rivers in a rainy season are allowed to flood the fields, and rice and other crops are planted as the floods recede. In other places, seasonal rainfall is stored in reservoirs for use in the dry season. Water may also be pumped from underground; this occurs particularly in the south-western USA and the Sahara.

In addition to flooding fields, water is fed to crops through channels, by spraying, or by drip feed from holes in pipes. The method used varies in cost and efficiency of water use: developing countries usually use channels in the soil, which are cheap but inefficient (much of the water is not used by the crop). Irrigation is especially important for these countries, which may have insufficient rainfall for agriculture and cannot afford to import food. Countries may also use large amounts of water for irrigation to grow high-value crops, such as fruit in the south-western USA.

If used inappropriately, irrigation can lead to a major problem — the salts present in the irrigation water can accumulate in the soil as the water evaporates, a process called **salinization**. This causes a decline in crop yields until eventually the soil becomes useless for agriculture. But it can be prevented by using enough irrigation water to wash the salts through the soil, and then draining this water from the fields.

Water is also used for transport, both on the sea and on rivers, lakes and canals. Most canals were built for transporting goods, sometimes linking navigable rivers. They are still important in parts of Europe, but the 3200 km of canals that were built in Britain during the late eighteenth and early nineteenth centuries are now little used, as goods can be moved more quickly by rail or road.

Recreational uses of water include angling, sailing and swimming, which can take place in reservoirs as well as in rivers, lakes and the sea. Water also has indirect uses: it provides salt and fish for food.

The uses of water can be divided into **abstractive uses**, where water is used in such a way as to be temporarily lost as a resource, and **non-abstractive uses** where water is used without major diversions from its natural path and without changing its quality. When water is used in industry, for example, this is an abstractive use; the use of water for recreation, such as sailing on a river, is non-abstractive.

○ Which of the following uses of water would you classify as abstractive, and which as non-abstractive? Domestic water supply; irrigation and other agricultural use; industrial manufacturing; cooling (industrial and electricity generation); hydroelectric power generation; transport; recreation.

○ The first four are abstractive uses. The last (cooling) is 'borderline', but in fact about 1% of cooling water is lost by evaporation and the rest is generally returned to the water source at a slightly higher temperature — its quality has changed. It is also diverted from its natural path. The last three are non-abstractive uses.

Where water resources are limited, rapid reuse may be possible. Power stations using cooling towers *recycle* water after cooling, with only a small amount lost through evaporation. Such a cooling system uses less water (about 1/50th) than the power stations without cooling towers, which return warmer water to the source without cooling it. Industry can also reuse water: steel production, for example, can use 5 to 200 litres per kilogram of steel, depending on the degree of reuse.

Substitution is possible for some uses of water, but not all uses have acceptable substitutes.

Activity 1

Consider the uses of water listed in the question above, and for each use comment on whether a substitute is possible, and what the substitute could be. What do you think is the major disadvantage of using substitutes for water?

1.2 Water in Britain

In England and Wales the Environment Agency has the responsibility for the management of water resources and the control and monitoring of water pollution. The Environment Agency also has responsibilities for flood defence, land drainage, fisheries, navigation, conservation and recreation in inland waters. It issues licences for abstractions of water and discharges of sewage and other effluents.

The public water supply ('tap water') is provided mainly by 10 water service companies (Figure 1) who supply about 75% of the population. The rest is supplied by 29 smaller water companies. The companies abstract water under licence from the Environment Agency. Sewage collection, treatment and disposal is also the responsibility of the water service companies.

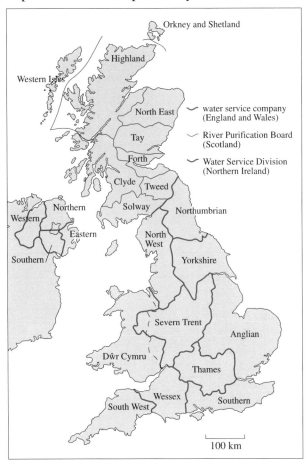

Figure 1 Water service company areas in England and Wales, River Purification Board areas in Scotland and Department of the Environment Water Service Division areas in Northern Ireland.

In Scotland, River Purification Boards are responsible for river management and pollution control (Figure 1), with water supply and sewerage being provided by the Regional and Island Councils.

In Northern Ireland a government department, the Department of the Environment, has the responsibility for water resources, pollution, supply and sewerage.

The quantities of fresh water used for various purposes are in Table 2. The public water supply is the water abstracted, purified and distributed through water mains to houses, offices, some industries and farms by the water companies. This accounts for about a half of all abstractions. The quantity generally increases each year, the 1990 supply being 13% more than that in 1980.

Water legislation in England and Wales

The management and control of water resources in England and Wales was altered considerably by the Water Act 1989, the Water Industry Act 1991, the Water Resources Act 1991 and the Environment Act 1995. The Water Authorities which existed prior to 1989 were restructured into new private sector water companies and water service companies (plcs). The acts also provided for the regulation of these companies, established new institutions to manage the water environment (the National Rivers Authority, the Drinking Water Inspectorate and Her Majesty's Inspectorate of Pollution; these were incorporated into the Environment Agency in 1995) and the water service companies (Director General of Water Services).

The Acts intend that the full cost of water and sewerage is met by the customers; this includes replacing old mains and sewers, and keeping to European Union regulations on water quality. In addition the private companies are expected to make a profit.

Table 2 The quantities of fresh water abstracted for different uses in England and Wales in 1990

Water use	Quantity/10^6 litres per day
public water supply	18 336
electricity generation	12 612
industry	3795
agriculture: spray irrigation	378
agriculture: other use	129
total	35 249

Values are averaged over a year. The value for electricity generation excludes brackish and salt water abstracted from estuaries and the sea but includes water used for hydroelectric power.

The other three types of users given in Table 2 get much of their water directly from rivers or the ground without going through the treatment works and distribution system of the public water supply. Industry, power stations and farms often do not require high-quality water, so it is cheaper to abstract water directly than to use the more expensive, high-quality public water supply. The direct abstraction of water is permitted only where it is licensed by the Environment Agency, which has to ensure that there is enough water available and that it will not affect other abstractions. For example, if an industry or power station takes water directly from a river, the Environment Agency has to make sure that there is still enough water in the river at all times, and will license abstraction only up to a certain quantity. Direct abstraction is not restricted to industry: in principle there is nothing to stop you digging a well in your garden for your own domestic water supply.

As Table 2 shows, after the public water supply, the largest use of water is for electricity generation. Because of the enormous quantities of water required, power stations are situated on major rivers, lakes or on the coast. The main use of water is for cooling, and this water can be of low quality. Even more water is obtained from estuaries (brackish water) and the sea (saline water). The water used for cooling is returned to the source relatively quickly but some 5 °C warmer. Some power stations recycle cooling water; this is not a continuous yearly demand but is a 'one-off' abstraction that stays within the cooling system and is never returned.

Another use of water in electricity generation is for raising steam in boilers, to convert thermal energy first to mechanical and then to electrical energy. Boilers require high-quality water, but this is much less than the amount used for cooling.

There are considerable year-to-year fluctuations in the amount of water used for electricity generation: in the 1980s it varied from a high of 13 087 million litres per day in 1980 to a low of 10 711 million litres per day in 1985.

Direct abstraction by industry generally reduced during the 1980s, falling by 42% between 1980 and 1988, after which it increased slightly. The main causes for the reduction were the more efficient use of water, including recycling, and changes in the structure of British industry, including the contraction of some of the major water-using industries, such as steel-making.

In England and Wales, agriculture consumes only a small proportion of the total water abstracted (Table 2), although, on a global scale, irrigation is the greatest use of water. There is sufficient rainfall for agriculture over Wales and the western and northern parts of England so irrigation is used mainly in the drier central, southern and eastern parts of England, particularly in East Anglia, and is not used regularly. Irrigation water is usually obtained by direct abstraction from rivers and boreholes and it can be of low quality. The quantity used for irrigation fluctuates widely from year to year, depending to a large extent on the weather. Abstractions were high in 1989 and 1990 due mainly to the hot, dry weather during the summer months. However, abstractions for the previous two years were only about a third of the 1989 and 1990 quantities. Although the quantity used for irrigation is relatively small in total, it tends to be highest in hot dry weather when water resources are most stretched. Also most of the irrigation water is lost to the atmosphere or underground, whereas water used for other purposes is eventually returned to rivers and can be rapidly reused.

In England and Wales, an average of 140 litres of water per person per day is used in the home (in comparison with the average of 500 litres per person per day for domestic, industrial and agricultural purposes in industrialized countries cited in Section 1.1). Figure 2 shows the different uses of this water. The domestic demand has grown from 36 litres per person per day at about the time of the last major cholera epidemic in London (1858) to 140 litres today because of improved living standards. Nearly all (99.2%) homes in England and Wales are now linked to the public water supply. Similar patterns of water use exist in other industrialized nations.

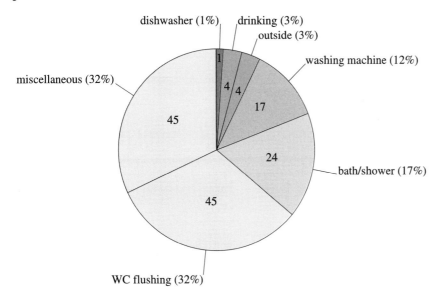

Figure 2 The use of water in an average household in England and Wales, 1990. The numbers on each segment give the volume in litres per person per day for each use. The 'miscellaneous' category includes water for cooking, cleaning and washing up. The 'outside' category includes water used in the garden and for car washing.

Activity 2

How does your water use compare with that in Figure 2? In this Activity you will measure how much water you use in one of these categories, that of bath/shower.

Over a period of a week, keep a record of how many baths and/or showers you had, and the duration of each shower.

Now work out how much water you use in an average bath, by measuring how long your bath taps take to fill a measuring jug or kettle, and how long the bath takes to run.

Now do the same for a shower, measuring how long it takes to fill the jug or kettle, so you can calculate the water use per minute of shower (as in Table 1).

Calculate your weekly water use for bath/shower, and finally your daily use averaged over a week. How does it compare with the average in Figure 2?

Question 2

Calculate the domestic consumption in England and Wales as a percentage of the public water supply for 1990. Take the average household consumption per person from this Section, the public water supply from Table 2 and the population as 50 million.

1.3 The economics of water

Water has traditionally been regarded as a free resource in the sense that there is nothing to stop anybody collecting their own supply of water from rainfall. Even water from the public supply is very cheap. Sand and gravel — the cheapest resources you have met so far — cost about £4.50 a tonne in the UK in 1993, compared with the average of 53 pence per tonne (a cubic metre) for mains water. However, some regions of the world are less fortunate. For example, in Kuwait most fresh water is produced by the expensive desalination of seawater, and there the cost of water is roughly comparable to the cost of oil.

Because water is generally cheap, it is uneconomic — or at any rate expensive — to transport water in large quantities very far from the source of supply; water is a resource with a high place value. There is effectively no world market in water, so what matters is local availability.

In previous Blocks of the Course we have discussed the price of resources in terms of supply and demand. In applying these concepts to water resources we need to bear three main points in mind:

1   A certain quantity of water is essential for life.

2   In most countries the water supply is under the control of a government organization or nationalized industry, so there is not a free market price for water, unlike in England and Wales.

3   The price of water depends on the source of supply.

We can work out the relationship between price and demand for water by first considering the desert island castaway. For the few litres a day necessary for survival, the castaway would give any price for the water, be it 53 pence or £53 per cubic metre, for without the water he or she would die. This small quantity of water is an essential amount so the water is inelastic in demand. As price comes down, water will be put to increasingly more uses, for the subsistence demands of cooking and some washing as well as drinking.

As the demand increases to the quantities used per person in developed countries, the situation becomes more complex, as different uses have different demand–price relationships. Consider domestic use. Relatively few British households have water meters, so the cost of water does not usually depend on the quantity of water used by any individual household. Therefore, people can use whatever quantity of water they wish and still pay the same flat rate for their water.

In the USA most houses have water meters, and so the cost depends on how much water is used. Small increases in price seem to have little effect on demand but large price increases do reduce demand. The quantity of water used in non-metered houses in the USA is about twice that used in metered houses. Metering trials in Britain have shown that after metering the demand fell by 10–15%. These findings suggest that the use of meters in domestic consumption leads to elasticity of demand. Similar considerations apply to the water used for industrial purposes, which is also metered. In recent years several industries have reduced their water bills by redesigning

Agricultural water in the south-western USA

The agricultural water supply in the south-western USA provides an illustration of the general principles of supply and demand. The soil and climate are very suitable for agriculture but the rainfall is low, so irrigation is necessary. To meet the demand for irrigation water, local rivers and underground water sources have been used, but these local supplies are insufficient for further agricultural development and water would have to be brought to the area from elsewhere. There is a surplus of water in states to the north of the area, but to transport this water would cost more than the value of the crops grown, so it is not economic to do so. However, if industry rather than agriculture were to expand in the south-western USA, it might become worth while to pay the high cost of transporting water to the area. This is a problem of water economics: water can be supplied to the south-western USA, but only at a high price, and to be economic the water would have to be used for expanding industry rather than agriculture.

manufacturing processes to use water more efficiently, and the electricity generating companies are making increasing use of recycled water for cooling.

The agricultural demand for water is very much influenced by price, so agricultural water is in elastic demand. A maximum price can be put on the water used for irrigation in terms of the selling price of the crops grown, and this maximum is usually quite low, less than the price that other users would be able to pay. For example, it takes 1000 litres of water to grow a kilogram of wheat or produce 5–20 kg of steel (Table 1); the steel would fetch a higher price than the wheat, so the steel industry could pay more for its water.

The relationship between price and supply for water is also variable. Small quantities of water might be obtained fairly easily and cheaply from a local river, and as long as there is water to be abstracted, a small change in price can produce a large change in supply: the supply is elastic. If the price is higher, wells can be drilled and underground water pumped to the surface. If the price becomes higher still, it becomes economic to pump water from greater depths, or an alternative supply of water may be used (for example, from a distant river or by desalination of seawater). The higher the price the water can fetch, the greater the incentive to supply a larger quantity.

1.4 Summary of Section 1

1 Water is a renewable resource; there is a virtually constant supply of fresh water, as water is recycled on the Earth.

2 A few litres of water per person per day are needed for survival. For subsistence, the daily requirement is 20–40 litres per person; this includes the use of water for cooking and washing in addition to drinking, but not water for growing food. Water use in industrialized countries is typically 500 litres per person per day. This includes water for various domestic purposes, industry, power generation and agriculture.

3 The largest use of water on a global scale is for agriculture (69%), most of which is for irrigation. On a global scale, 8% of water is used for domestic purposes, and 23% for industry.

4 The uses of water can be separated into abstractive and non-abstractive ones. An abstractive use is where water is used in such a way as to be temporarily lost as a resource, as when used for the domestic water supply. In a non-abstractive use, such as transport, neither the natural route nor the quality of the water is changed.

5   In Britain the public water supply accounts for the most fresh water. The average domestic demand is 140 litres per person per day, which takes between a third and a half of the public water supply. Electricity generation also requires large quantities of fresh water, and even larger quantities of water from estuaries and the sea. Irrigation uses only a small proportion of the water abstracted in Britain, but does so at a time of greatest demand on water resources.

6   In the UK, water is the cheapest of all physical resources, at an average of 53p per tonne (1993). Supply and demand relationships apply to water as they do to other resources. Water generally has a high place value, as the cost of transporting water adds considerably to its price.

Question 3

Why is the use of water for hydroelectric power regarded as non-abstractive, whereas the use of water for cooling during electricity generation is mainly regarded as abstractive?

Question 4

In Section 1.1 it was stated that in industrialized countries about 500 litres of water are used per person per day. Using the population figure in Question 2 and the total amount of water abstracted daily (Table 2), calculate the average amount of water per person used daily in England and Wales, and comment on your answer.

2 THE WATER CYCLE

Water moves over, on and through the Earth in a continuous cycle driven by the Sun and gravity. It is known as the **water cycle** or the **hydrological cycle** (shown in blue in Figure 3). The cycle involves water: as a liquid, a solid (ice and snow) and a gas (water vapour). Water can take many different paths through the cycle. The total volume of water in the water cycle remains virtually constant. There are two main types of water in the cycle:

1   **meteoric water**, which is fresh water derived by condensation from the atmosphere and which accumulates as surface water (rivers and freshwater lakes) and underground water;

2   *saline water*, the seawater of the oceans and some lakes.

Small amounts of **magmatic water** from the interior of the Earth are *added* to the cycle by volcanic eruptions. **Formation water**, on the other hand, is water that is trapped within the pores of sediment, and to all purposes is *removed* from the water cycle. This can be either water that was originally trapped in the sediments during their formation, or water that percolated into the rocks later. Formation water is usually saline, mainly because the water originally trapped in the sediments was often seawater.

Figure 3   The water, or hydrological, cycle. Water cycles (blue arrows) between reservoirs (boxes) of the hydrosphere. Surface runoff is defined in Section 4.1.

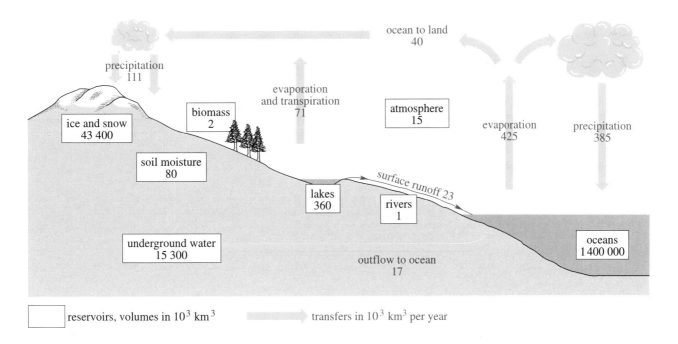

2.1 Storage of water in the hydrosphere

The **hydrosphere** includes the parts of the Earth that are mainly water, such as the oceans, icecaps, lakes and rivers. Various parts of the hydrosphere can be seen on the Block cover illustration. This is a mosaic, compiled from a number of satellite images, to give a view of the Earth almost unobstructed by clouds. The oceans and lakes are blue; and snow and ice are white in the icecaps of the Arctic, Antarctic and Greenland, and on high mountains such as the Himalayas. (The yellow and brown areas are deserts, and vegetation appears green.)

All parts of the hydrosphere store water temporarily, and are called reservoirs. These natural reservoirs of the hydrosphere are not to be confused with the human-built reservoirs used to store water on land: for example, the atmosphere is a reservoir, containing $15 \times 10^3 \, km^3$ of water. The study of water movement upon and beneath the ground and the physics and chemistry of the water is called **hydrology**.

- What are the main ways in which water is transferred between the various reservoirs of the hydrosphere shown in Figure 3?

- Evaporation and transpiration, precipitation, surface runoff and outflow of underground water to the ocean.

The average length of time that water stays in a reservoir before moving to another reservoir is called the **residence time** for that reservoir (Table 3). A hydrosphere reservoir empties and replenishes at the same rate, and the residence time is calculated from the rate of movement of water in relation to the volume of the reservoir. There may be several ways in which water is transferred to and from a reservoir (Figure 3).

$$\text{residence time} = \frac{\text{volume in reservoir}}{\text{rate of transfer from or to reservoir}}$$

For example, the residence time for rivers:

$$= \frac{1 \times 10^3 \, km^3 \text{ (from Table 3)}}{23 \times 10^3 \, y^{-1} \text{ (from Figure 3)}}$$

$$= 0.043 \text{ years (about 2 weeks)}$$

Residence time is a concept that can be applied to any cyclical process, not just the water cycle. Figure 3 shows that the transfers of the cycle are in balance: in particular, water lost to the atmosphere by evaporation and transpiration is balanced by water returned by precipitation. The residence time gives an indication of how quickly water in a hydrosphere reservoir can be renewed. The shortest residence time, 11 days, is for water vapour in the atmosphere, which is continually renewed by evaporation from the oceans and land and lost by precipitation. This is a rapid *subcycle* of the water cycle. Subcycles involving the oceans, the icecaps and underground water are much slower (Table 3).

There is a large volume of fresh water locked up in the polar icecaps (Table 3), but these are far from the centres of population and the arid countries that need it. It is not economic to transport this water at the moment, but it may become so in the future (Section 7.6).

Table 3 Amounts and residence times for water in the water cycle

Reservoir	Volume of water/$10^3 \, km^3$	Percentage of total water	Residence time
ocean	1 400 000	95.9	about 3000 years
polar icecaps	43 400	3.0	about 10 000 years
underground water	15 300	1.0	a few weeks to 10 000 years
lakes	360	0.025	about 10 years
soil moisture	80	0.005	a few weeks to 1 year
atmosphere	15	0.001	about 11 days
rivers	1	0.000 07	a few weeks

Apart from the oceans and icecaps, the greatest volume of water is underground, stored in porous rocks below the Earth's surface. The shallower underground water moves quite quickly through the cycle and is fresh water, so it can be used for water resources. But it is only a small proportion of the total underground water, and its residence time is relatively short, ranging from a few weeks to a few years. Underground water below a depth of a few hundred metres moves more slowly through the cycle, and residence times are much longer, up to thousands of years (Table 3). Much of this water is saline either because it is warmer, or has had time to dissolve salts from the rocks, or it retains a saline component derived from seawater.

The world's lakes contain large volumes of water (Table 3) and are more accessible than the polar icecaps. However, over half of these lakes are saline, and 80% of the water in the freshwater lakes occurs in only forty large lakes, including the Great Lakes of North America ($32 \times 10^3 \, km^3$) and Lake Baikal in Asia ($22 \times 10^3 \, km^3$). Rivers are very useful for water resources. They store very little water (Table 3), but the water in them is rapidly renewed — it has a short residence time of a few weeks.

The water found underground and in the icecaps, lakes and rivers forms about 4% of the total water in the cycle; but because the deeper underground water, the icecaps and the saline lakes are not a usable source of water at the moment, the amount of water that can be used for water resources is much less, only about 1% of the total.

Question 5

The amount of fresh water that can theoretically be exploited is determined by the excess of precipitation over evaporation and transpiration on land. Calculate this annual excess from Figure 3.

The answer to Question 5 may seem a large quantity of water, but this water is distributed very unevenly, as can be seen from the extensive water shortages and droughts in many parts of the world. In order to understand the problems of availability and distribution of water in more detail, we shall now look at the processes in the water cycle that transfer water between the hydrosphere reservoirs.

2.2 Precipitation

Water in the atmosphere, although it is one of the smallest reservoirs, is the most important source of water. It exists as vapour, liquid (clouds and raindrops) or in solid form (snow and ice). When air rises (as it will, for example, when it moves over mountains) it expands, owing to the decrease in pressure, and as it expands it cools at an average rate of 1 °C per 100 metres of altitude. As the air cools, water vapour condenses around small particles suspended in the air, such as pollen grains, fungal spores, dust and salt from sea spray. This condensation results in the formation of clouds composed of droplets of moisture from 0.001 mm to 0.1 mm in diameter. Precipitation of this water to the Earth's surface occurs when these droplets coalesce to form larger drops about 1 mm in diameter, or when ice crystals form. Precipitation may be in the form of rain, snow or hail. Water vapour may also precipitate by condensing directly onto the land surface as dew or hoar frost.

under 250 mm

250 to 500 mm

500 to 1000 mm

1000 to 2000 mm

over 2000 mm

Figure 4 Average annual precipitation on land.

The net effect of the water cycle is to transfer some $40 \times 10^3 \, km^3$ of fresh water each year from the oceans to the land by precipitation, as calculated in Question 5 and shown in Figure 3. Globally, precipitation is distributed very unevenly in both position and time. Figure 4 shows the global distribution of precipitation on land. Some areas get less than 250 mm annually (precipitation is usually measured in millimetres); such areas are usually deserts, such as in the Middle East, North Africa, north-central Asia and central Australia. These are visible as the yellow/buff areas on the Block cover. The annual rainfall in other areas may reach as much as 12 000 mm; this heavy rainfall is characteristic of the Amazon Basin and parts of South and South-East Asia. These areas are green on the cover. Precipitation can vary in amount from year to year, and in many regions it is seasonal, as on the Indian subcontinent where the south-west monsoon brings rain for a few months in the summer only. Irregular rainfall is common in drier areas, where rain may fall for only a few days each year; the equivalent of a year's rain may occur in one storm lasting a few hours.

The yearly irregularity of rainfall in some areas can be seen in Figure 5, which contrasts the rainfall for Niamey, a town in sub-Saharan Africa (the Sahel) with that for England and Wales.

Question 6

(a) What is the range (minimum and maximum) of annual precipitation for (i) Niamey in 1905–87; (ii) England and Wales in 1979–91?

(b) What is the minimum annual precipitation as a percentage of the mean annual precipitation for (i) Niamey; (ii) England and Wales?

Areas such as the Sahel, with a fairly low rainfall and the high variability shown in Figure 5a, are classed as semi-arid, and are vulnerable to drought in years of lower than average rainfall.

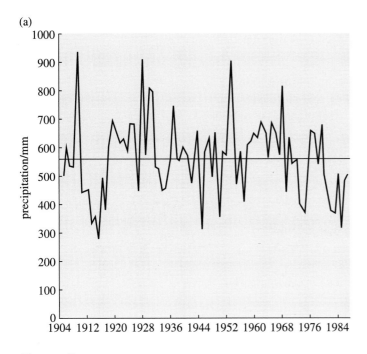
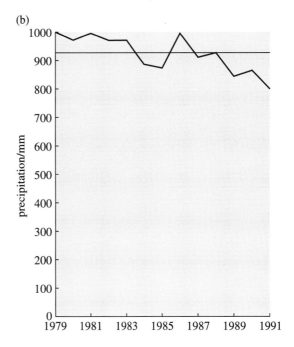

Figure 5 Annual precipitation values for (a) Niamey, in Niger, for 1905–87; (b) England and Wales for 1979–91. The vertical scale is the same for both. The horizontal lines are the mean annual precipitation during these periods: 562 mm for Niamey, and 925 mm for England and Wales.

Activity 3

There have been reports of drought conditions in the Sahel since the early 1970s. Explain whether the data in Figure 5a provide evidence for a period of lower rainfall since 1970 and whether there is evidence for a longer term decrease in rainfall.

Another difference in precipitation between the Sahel and England and Wales is the seasonality of the Sahel rain: England and Wales have rain spread throughout the year, whereas Niamey averages only 44 rainy days a year, confined to a rainy season (Figure 6).

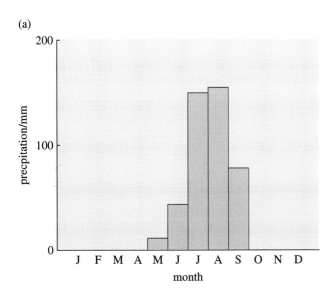
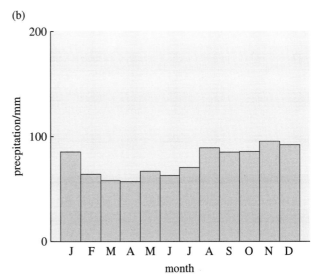

Figure 6 Monthly precipitation values for (a) Niamey, for 1980; precipitation occurs in the summer months of May to September only; (b) England and Wales, average 1951–80; precipitation occurs throughout the year.

Niamey, and England and Wales are in different global precipitation regimes (Table 4). Each regime has a characteristic annual precipitation and seasonal pattern (Figure 7).

Because of the prevailing westerly winds, Britain's precipitation is more evenly distributed throughout the year (Figures 6 and 7), and more constant from year to year (Figure 5b), than that of many other countries. The amount

Table 4 Global precipitation regimes

A *Equatorial* Within a few degrees N and S of Equator	rain all year, 1 or 2 seasons
B *Tropical* Between Equator and Tropics of Cancer and Capricorn	summer rain, winter dry
(1) Inner zone, to 10° N and S	two summer maxima
(2) Outer zone, 10° N and S to the Tropics	single summer maximum, longer dry season
C *Monsoon* Within and outside the Tropics in the Indian subcontinent, on the east side	high summer maximum, long dry season
D *Subtropical* Tropics to 30° N and S on the west side of continents	dry: desert areas
At the margins: Poleward (30° latitude) Equatorward (23.5° latitude)	winter rain summer rain
E *Mediterranean* Within 30° to 40° N and S on the west side of continents	winter rain, summer dry
F *Mid-latitudes*	precipitation at all seasons
G *Polar*	precipitation at all seasons, in very small amounts

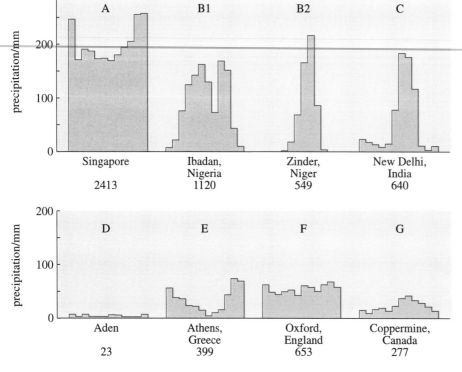

Figure 7 Monthly precipitation patterns for the global precipitation regimes in Table 4. The number below each histogram is the average annual precipitation in millimetres.

of precipitation does, however, vary from place to place. In the east of England the average annual precipitation is about 500 mm, although in mountainous parts of north-west Scotland, the Lake District and northern Wales the precipitation is over 2500 mm (Figure 8).

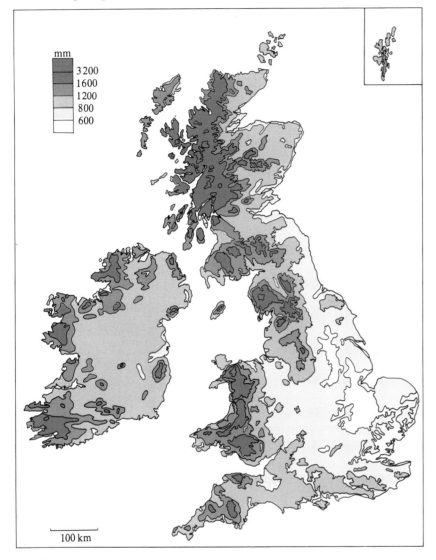

mm
3200
1600
1200
800
600

100 km

Figure 8 The mean annual precipitation in the British Isles, 1941–70.

⬤ Why is there such a difference in precipitation in different parts of Britain?

⬤ The regional variation is caused by differences in altitude and in the paths of atmospheric depressions (low-pressure regions; often called 'weather systems') over Britain.

When air rises, it cools, causing precipitation, and this occurs when the westerly airstreams are deflected upward over coastal mountains in Scotland, the Lake District and Wales, which are the wettest parts of mainland Britain, or when warm air rises over cold air at the edge of a depression. More depressions pass across the north of Britain than the south, so the north is wetter. There is an uneven distribution of precipitation in Britain in relation to population density; the sparsely inhabited mountainous areas, with the lowest demands for water, have the highest precipitation. Although the precipitation in Britain is fairly evenly spread throughout the year, evaporation is much higher in the summer. In the densely inhabited regions of England with low precipitation, it is necessary to store water in the winter for use in the summer, otherwise the supply would not be sufficient.

Question 7

(a) The area of England is $130\,470\,km^2$ and that of Wales is $20\,760\,km^2$; their average annual precipitation values are 837 mm and 1385 mm, respectively. What is the total volume of water that falls on England and Wales annually?

(b) What percentage of this water was abstracted in 1990? (Use Table 2).

Question 7 seems to imply a high rate of use of water resources. Such a rate would be catastrophic for most physical resources, but not for water, as it is a renewable resource that is used, often many times, as it passes through the water cycle from rainfall to the ocean. Even when it is temporarily lost as a freshwater resource, in the oceans or deep underground, it is renewable in a few thousand years — a faster timescale than most of the other physical resources in this Course. The purpose of most of our intervention in the water cycle is to slow down the rate at which water reaches the ocean, such as by trapping river water in reservoirs to be used when we need it.

2.3 Interception, evaporation and transpiration

Most of the precipitation reaches the ground, but not all of it, as some is stopped by vegetation above the ground, a process known as **interception**. This is part of a subcycle of the water cycle, which involves precipitation, interception and evaporation back to the atmosphere, bypassing that part of the main cycle where water reaches the surface of the ground.

The proportion of the precipitation stopped, the **interception loss**, depends on the type of vegetation, its age, density of planting and the season of the year. The interception loss in forested areas is 25–35% for coniferous forests and 15–25% for broad-leaved forests (values averaged over a year). In grassland it is usually lower, 14–19% for natural grasses. Crops have highly variable values — about 7% for oats, 16% for corn and about 40% for clover, for example. In arid and semi-arid areas, where there is little vegetation, the interception loss can be as low as 1%.

Water that reaches the ground without being intercepted may become part of the **overland flow** (water flowing across the ground surface), or it may soak into the soil and underlying rocks, or evaporate. Evaporation is the process by which water is transferred from the land or ocean to the atmosphere. The rate of evaporation increases with temperature. The process also depends on the **humidity** (a measure of how close the air is to saturation with water vapour) and the wind speed. The greater the humidity, the less the evaporation. Wind carries water-saturated air away from the surface, so wind decreases the local humidity and allows more water to evaporate.

The rate of evaporation is highest from open water. Over the ground surface the rate of evaporation depends on the type of soil and the extent to which the ground is saturated with water. If the ground is saturated just below the surface, water can move up to the surface by **capillary action**. In this process water tends to cling to the walls of narrow openings and hence to move upwards through interconnected small spaces. The amount of capillary rise depends on the size of the pore spaces and the number of interconnected pores. It is generally greater for small pore spaces than for larger ones. Evaporation from a saturated sandy soil can take place nearly as quickly as it can from open water, whereas evaporation from a saturated clay soil is slower, between 75% and 90% of the rate from open water. This is because although the pore spaces in clays are smaller, they are less interconnected and so water moves slowly through clays. (We shall deal with this more fully in Section 3.5.)

Figure 9 shows how evaporation and precipitation vary with latitude. Over two-thirds of the total global evaporation occurs within 30° of the Equator, because of the higher temperatures in equatorial and tropical areas. Evaporation reaches its greatest values not at the Equator, but between 10° and 20° in both hemispheres, because of the strong trade winds at these latitudes. This water vapour is carried towards the Equator by the trade winds, giving a very high precipitation in the equatorial zone where the trade-wind systems converge.

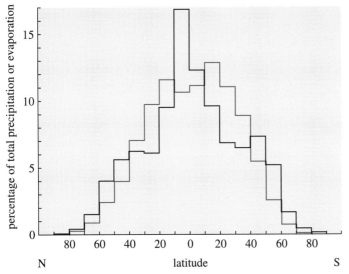

Figure 9 The latitudinal distribution of annual precipitation (black) and annual evaporation (blue), expressed in terms of the percentage of the total global precipitation or evaporation within each ten-degree latitude belt.

Evaporation also varies with season, because of its dependence on temperature and humidity. In Britain, for example, evaporation is very low in winter and highest in summer (Figure 10).

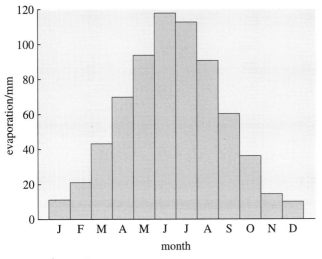

Figure 10 Average monthly evaporation for Kempton Park reservoir, in the Thames valley, 1956–62.

Question 8

(a) How much greater is the evaporation in summer (June) than in winter (December) at Kempton Park?

(b) Is this similar to the difference in precipitation between summer and winter in England?

So although precipitation in England (and the rest of Britain) is not very seasonal, the *availability of water* is due in large part to the extreme seasonality of evaporation.

Vegetation also increases the amount of water returned to the air by **transpiration**. This is the process by which water is drawn from the soil by plant roots and transferred to the leaves, from which it evaporates through pores in the leaf system. It is controlled essentially by the factors that affect evaporation, and by the type of plant. A considerable amount of water can be transferred to the atmosphere by transpiration: for example, a cabbage transpires about 25 litres of water during its growth to full size, and a large oak tree transpires about 400 litres of water a day when in leaf.

Evaporation and transpiration are difficult parts of the hydrological cycle to quantify, as it is hard to measure the transfer to water vapour directly. Over land areas it is also difficult to separate the effects of evaporation and transpiration, so the two are usually combined into one parameter, called **evapotranspiration**. It is relatively easy to calculate a maximum value of evapotranspiration for a saturated surface, such as open water, using local meteorological parameters such as humidity, temperature and wind speed. This is called the **potential evapotranspiration** for a particular area. It is the maximum possible evapotranspiration that could take place given an unlimited supply of moisture. Because most land surfaces are neither open water nor saturated, and are partly or wholly covered in vegetation, values of evapotranspiration are always less than potential evapotranspiration.

In Britain, values of annual potential evapotranspiration increase from a minimum of 356 mm in the north to a maximum of 584 mm in the south (Figure 11).

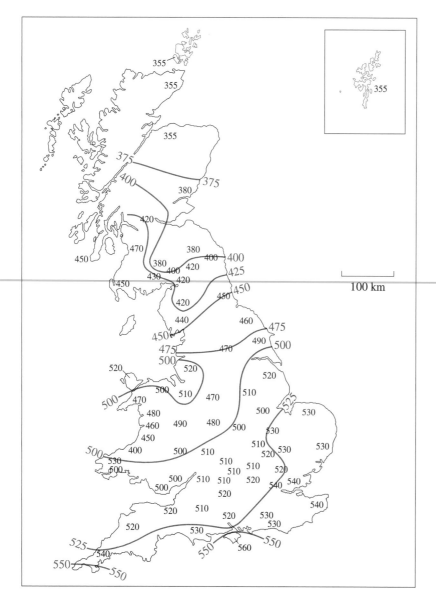

Figure 11 Annual potential evapotranspiration in Britain (values in mm).

○ Are the areas of greatest precipitation in Britain also the areas of greatest potential evapotranspiration?

○ No. The areas of greatest precipitation in Britain are the west of Scotland, the Lake District and North Wales (Figure 8), whereas the greatest potential evapotranspiration is in the south.

○ Is the potential evapotranspiration in Britain greater or less than the precipitation?

○ In Britain and other places with a temperate climate the potential (and actual) evapotranspiration is less than the precipitation.

This is true only on an annual basis, as evapotranspiration is much higher in summer than in winter. Evapotranspiration is usually greater than precipitation in the summer months, and less than precipitation in winter (Figure 12). The precipitation that is not evaporated or transpired back to the atmosphere either soaks into the ground or becomes overland flow. A rough indication of the quantity of water available from underground or from rivers in any area is given by the excess of precipitation over actual evapotranspiration, as we calculated in Question 5. Because underground water and surface water are very important for water resources, they are examined in more detail in the next two Sections.

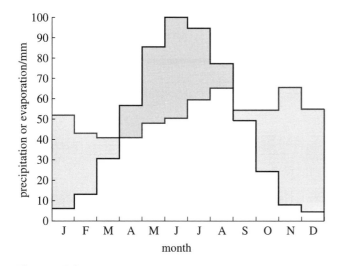

Figure 12 Precipitation (blue line) and potential evapotranspiration (black line) in the Anglian water company region. The blue shading represents the excess of precipitation over potential evapotranspiration in the winter months and the grey shading represents a greater potential evapotranspiration than precipitation in the summer months.

There are also many areas of the world where the potential evapotranspiration is greater than the precipitation — usually hot areas where precipitation is low (Figure 4). In parts of North Africa and the Middle East the precipitation may be less than 50 mm a year, but the potential evapotranspiration is about 3000 mm a year. However, the actual evapotranspiration in these areas is much less than potential evapotranspiration because there is usually little water to be evaporated. The water resources problems in these areas are illustrated by a study of water in one arid country, Jordan, in Section 6.2.

We have now completed a preliminary look at the water cycle, and this is the place to listen to Audio Band 5: *The Water Cycle*. You will need to have this Block open at Figure 3 and also refer to Table 3. The audiovisual sequence is a consolidation of the material in this Section, to help an understanding of the processes in the water cycle, as this is fundamental to the discussion of the past, present and future use of water resources. If you found Section 2 fairly easy you should be able to complete this AV quickly, in about 20 minutes, but if you found the Section difficult, go through the AV slowly, so that you understand the processes in the water cycle, before starting the next Section.

2.4 Summary of Section 2

1   The water cycle involves the movement of water, in all its forms, over, on and through the rocks near the surface of the Earth in a cycle. This cycle is driven by the Sun's energy and the Earth's gravity. The total volume of water in the cycle is virtually constant. Magmatic water adds small amounts of water to the cycle, and formation water removes small amounts of water from the cycle. Water is stored in reservoirs of the hydrosphere: in the oceans, underground, in the icecaps, and in lakes, rivers, the soil and the atmosphere. There is a transfer of water to the oceans by surface runoff (see Section 4.2 for an explanation) and outflow of underground water.

2   The residence time for water in a reservoir is the average length of time that water remains in that reservoir. It is calculated by dividing the volume in storage by the rate of transfer to or from another part of the cycle. Residence time is a measure of the rate at which water in different parts of the cycle is renewed: it is fastest in the atmosphere (11 days) and rivers (a few weeks). Only about 4% of the water in the water cycle is not seawater. The proportion of fresh water which can be used for water supplies is less than this, about 1% of the total.

3   Precipitation has a very uneven global distribution, but is greatest near the Equator. On a smaller scale, precipitation is greatest over mountainous areas on land. Interception is the process by which precipitation is prevented from reaching the ground by vegetation.

4   Water is returned to the atmosphere by evaporation and transpiration. Transpiration is the process by which water is drawn from the soil by plant roots, transferred to the leaves and then evaporates. Evaporation and transpiration can be combined into one parameter, evapotranspiration. A maximum theoretical value for evapotranspiration, called potential evapotranspiration, can be calculated from meteorological parameters for any area.

Question 9

Which part of the hydrosphere has the greatest *range* of residence times, and why?

Question 10

Figure 9 shows that evaporation from the Earth's surface is greater in the southern hemisphere than in the northern hemisphere. Suggest an explanation for this.

3 GROUNDWATER

3.1 Water underground

Many people have the impression that underground water occupies vast caverns, such as those in the Derbyshire Peak District, flowing from one cavern to another along underground rivers. This is a popular misconception: underground caverns are fairly rare, but water does exist commonly underground, *within* rocks. This is because rocks usually contain pores, spaces that come in all shapes and sizes. In sediments there are pores between grains (Figure 13 and Plate 30) which can be filled with water. There may also be spaces between bedding planes or along joints, fractures or fissures which can also contain water (Figure 14). However, before we look at pores in more detail we will examine how water gets into the rock.

Figure 13 An electron microscope photograph of a sandstone. Pores make up 31% of the rock's volume. The largest grains are about 0.5 mm long.

Figure 14 Spaces resulting from bedding planes, joints, fractures and fissures in a limestone cliff face.

3.2 Infiltration

Precipitation that reaches the ground either runs off at the surface, or sinks into it. **Infiltration** is the movement of water through the ground surface into the soil and on downwards. The rate at which infiltration can take place depends, among other things, on the **permeability** of the soil or rock. Permeability is a measure of the ease with which water can move through soil or rock: the greater the permeability, the easier the infiltration. We shall deal with permeability more fully in Section 3.6. The total amount of infiltration also depends on the time available for water to seep into the ground. Heavy rainfall usually results in rapid overland flow, and relatively little infiltration into the ground.

Question 11

What effect will each of (a)–(e) have upon the total amount of infiltration, and why?

(a) dense vegetation,

(b) steeply sloping land surface,

(c) bare soil,

(d) roads and buildings,

(e) frozen subsoil.

There are two distinct zones beneath the ground surface (Figure 15). The **aeration zone** has mainly air-filled pores, with water held by surface tension in a film around the soil or rock particles. Water moves through this zone, into the **saturated zone** beneath, in which all the pores are filled with water. The **water table** is the level of water in a well, and is the boundary surface between the saturated zone and aeration zone. Water below the water table, in the saturated zone, is **groundwater**. Just above the water table is the **capillary zone**, in which there is some upward movement of water from the saturated zone by capillary action.

The thickness of the aeration zone depends mainly on the climate, but also on the topography (Section 3.3). In arid and mountainous regions this zone may be hundreds of metres thick, whereas in areas of high rainfall it may be only a few metres thick. There is no aeration zone beneath swamps, lakes or rivers, where the saturated zone extends to the surface. The thickness of the

Figure 15 Underground water. (a) The infiltration process, the aeration zone, the saturated zone and groundwater. (b) Where water is held in each zone.

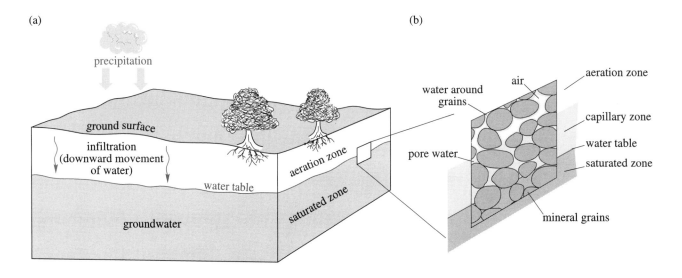

capillary zone will depend on the soil or rock texture, from a few millimetres in gravel to several metres in chalk or clay and sometimes this zone may reach the surface. The saturated zone extends downwards as far as the permeability of the rock will allow, a few tens of metres in some places, a kilometre or more in others. Water movement in the saturated zone is predominantly *sideways* (unlike in the aeration zone, where it is mainly *downwards*).

3.3 The water table

The water table, the boundary between the aeration zone and the saturated zone, is the level at which water stands in wells, and is a fundamental reference surface in the study of groundwater. It tends to follow the ground surface, rising under hills and falling at valleys, but the gradient of the water table is usually much less than that of the ground surface (Figure 16). Under hills the water table is usually at greater depths below the surface than it is below valleys. Where the rocks are very permeable, water can flow through them easily, so the water table will be more nearly horizontal. Where the water table intersects the surface of the ground (Figure 16c), groundwater will flow out at the surface as springs, or to streams or rivers.

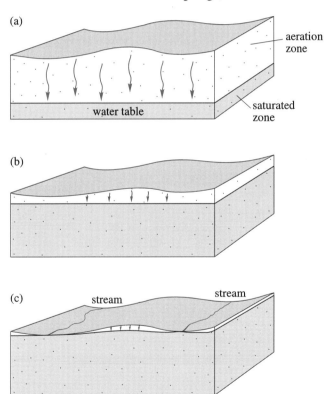

Figure 16 The water table. As water sinks into the ground, the water table rises as a horizontal plane in (a) and (b), until it reaches the ground surface in the valleys in (c), where groundwater seeps out as springs and to streams on the surface and the water table is no longer horizontal or planar.

The water table can be mapped from the level of the water in wells (in the same way as topographic contours, lines joining places with the same elevation, can be drawn from the height of the ground surface), so the level of the water table can be predicted where there are no wells. Figure 17a is a map of an outcrop of Triassic sandstones in part of Nottinghamshire, showing both the ground surface and water table contours. Figure 17b is a N–S cross-section across the area in Figure 17a.

(a)

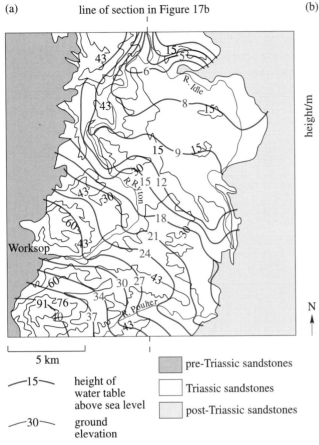

(b)

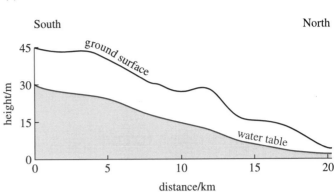

Figure 17 (a) A water table map for the Triassic sandstones in part of Nottinghamshire. The topographic ground surface contours are shown in black and the water table contours in blue. Higher areas of the ground surface and areas where the water table rises have higher contour values. Contours are given in metres above sea level. (b) A N–S cross-section of the outcrop of the Triassic sandstones in (a).

Question 12

Answer the questions (a) to (d), using Figure 17.

(a) Is the water table nearer to the surface of the ground in the northern or southern part of the area?

(b) What is the general direction of the slope of the water table?

(c) What is the relationship between undulations in the water table and the topography?

(d) At what depth below the surface of the ground will the water table be found on the highest ground in the figure (3 km south of Worksop)?

The general slope of the water table in Figure 17 is in the same direction as the slope of the ground surface, and undulations of the water table follow undulations of the ground. The water table does not, however, slope as steeply as the ground surface.

The water table has a seasonal rise and fall. There is a lag between the time of maximum infiltration and the highest water table level. In Britain, for example, the highest rates of infiltration occur in the winter but the water table does not reach its highest level until spring, because infiltration is a relatively slow process, and it takes time for water to reach the saturated zone.

3.4 Groundwater movement

Groundwater flows underground in response to pressure gradients, from an area of high pressure to an area of low pressure. Near the water table, this means that groundwater usually flows 'downhill', i.e. from a higher level to a lower level, just as it would on the surface. The difference in pressure between two points that are a horizontal distance l metres apart on a sloping water table is determined by the difference in height (h) between them (Figure 18). This height is called the **head** of water. The slope of the water table is called the **hydraulic gradient** and is defined as h/l. The equation that relates the speed of groundwater movement (v) to the hydraulic gradient is known as **Darcy's law**:

$$v = K \frac{h}{l} \tag{3.1}$$

In Equation 3.1, K is the **hydraulic conductivity** and is defined as the volume of water that will flow through a unit cross-sectional area of the rock per unit time, under a unit hydraulic gradient and at a specified temperature. The units of hydraulic conductivity are metres per second (m s^{-1}) or metres per day.

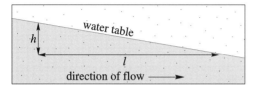

Figure 18 The flow of water through a permeable rock below the water table; h is the head of water over a horizontal distance l, so that h/l is the hydraulic gradient.

The hydraulic conductivity depends on the properties of the rock that allow water to flow through it (its permeability) and also on the properties of the water. Unlike hydraulic conductivity, permeability is an intrinsic property of the rock, so it is the same whatever the nature of the fluid flowing through the rock — whether water as in this instance, or oil and gas. The hydraulic conductivity (K), however, depends on the density and viscosity of water, so it will vary with the prevailing conditions. The most important factor that affects it is temperature. For example, an increase in water temperature from 5 °C to about 30 °C will double the hydraulic conductivity and, from Darcy's law, will therefore double the speed at which the groundwater flows.

Rocks can be divided into two broad categories — permeable and impermeable — on the basis of their hydraulic conductivity. Rocks regarded as permeable have hydraulic conductivities of 1 m per day or more. Rocks with hydraulic conductivities of less than 10^{-3} m per day are usually regarded as impermeable.

So how fast does water flow underground? The answer is: extremely slowly, in comparison with surface flow, even for rocks with high hydraulic conductivities. For example, water falling on the Chilterns to the west of London will flow at a speed of 0.1 to 1 m s^{-1} in a river, taking a few days to reach London. However, groundwater, even flowing through rocks with hydraulic conductivities as high as 1 m per day, will only have a speed of

Henri Darcy

Darcy's law is named after Henri Darcy, who was born in Dijon in France in 1803. He trained as an engineer, and worked to solve the problem of providing drinking water in Dijon, which at the time had no reliable and safe supply. Darcy designed a water supply system for the city from a large spring 10 km away, piped to standpipes in the city, providing Dijon with its first good water supply.

Darcy also carried out experiments into the science of water flow and derived the relationship between the speed of flow and the hydraulic gradient which is now known as Darcy's law. This was published in 1856, together with his work on water supply, under the title *Les Fontaines Publiques de la Ville de Dijon*.

around 3×10^{-3} m per day under the hydraulic gradient from the Chilterns to London, and will take thousands of years to travel the same distance.

The hydraulic conductivity is proportional to the permeability (permeability is discussed in greater detail in Section 3.6). So from Darcy's law (Equation 3.1) it can be deduced that in a rock of constant hydraulic conductivity (K), and hence of constant permeability for a given fluid, the speed (v) at which the groundwater flows will increase as the hydraulic gradient (h/l, the slope of the water table) increases.

Groundwater flows in the general direction of maximum slope of the water table, at least for groundwater near the top of the saturated zone. This means that the direction in which groundwater flows can be deduced from contour maps of the water table, as the direction of maximum slope is at right-angles to the water table contours. In Figure 19 we have added directions of flow to the water table contour map in Figure 17a. In Question 12 we deduced that the water table in this area sloped down to the north-east, so the direction of groundwater flow is also to the north-east.

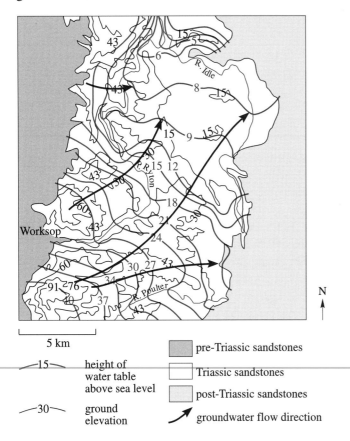

5 km

—15— height of water table above sea level

—30— ground elevation

▨ pre-Triassic sandstones

☐ Triassic sandstones

▨ post-Triassic sandstones

➚ groundwater flow direction

N ↑

Figure 19 Direction of groundwater flow in the Triassic sandstones in Nottinghamshire. This figure covers the same area as Figure 17. The groundwater flows at right-angles to the water table contours, i.e. in the direction of slope of the water table.

This flow of groundwater in the direction of the slope of the water table is only part of the picture, for groundwater is also in motion at greater depths, where it generally moves in a curved path rather than a straight line when seen in cross-section (Figure 20), towards a stream or river, a spring, or even a well. This path is the result of movement towards an area with a lower head of pressure, such as the stream.

It is often useful to measure the flow of groundwater in terms of the volume of water instead of its speed. Volume and speed are related by the equation

$$Q = Av \tag{3.2}$$

where Q is the volume of water flowing in unit time, at speed v, through a section of rock of cross-sectional area A. (Note that Q is the *rate* of flow, measured as volume per unit time.) Darcy's law can be substituted into this

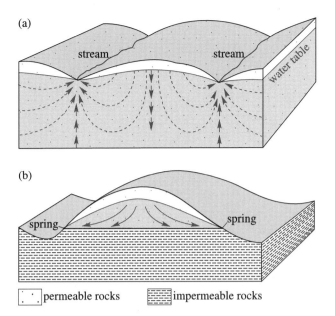

(a)

stream stream water table

(b)

spring spring

permeable rocks   impermeable rocks

Figure 20 The direction of flow of groundwater at depth is not parallel to the water table; instead, water moves in a curved path, converging towards a point of discharge. In (a) the rock is uniformly permeable, and the water discharges into streams in the valleys; it may approach the stream from below. In (b) the hill is capped by a permeable rock which is underlain by an impermeable rock. The water is diverted laterally by the impermeable rock, and springs result where the boundary between the permeable and impermeable rocks intersects the ground surface.

equation to give the volume in terms of hydraulic conductivity and hydraulic gradient:

$$Q = AK \frac{h}{l} \tag{3.3}$$

In addition to the natural discharge at streams, rivers or springs, groundwater can be extracted from wells. The water table around a well from which water is being pumped will fall, forming a **cone of depression** (Figure 21). The shape and extent of the cone of depression depend on the hydraulic conductivity of the rock, the rate of pumping, and the duration of pumping. The difference in height between the water table before pumping and the level of water in the well during pumping is called the **drawdown**.

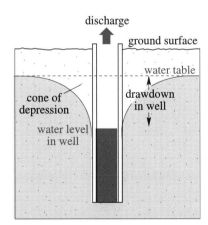

discharge

ground surface

water table

cone of depression

drawdown in well

water level in well

Figure 21 The water table is drawn down into a cone of depression around a pumped well.

At a coast, groundwater discharges into the sea under normal conditions because the water table slopes down towards sea level (Figure 22). Rocks under the sea generally have saline groundwater in them, derived from seawater. The boundary between fresh groundwater and saline groundwater usually slopes down inland from the coast, with a wedge of more dense saline groundwater under the less dense fresh groundwater below the land. The depth below sea level of the interface between fresh and saline groundwater at any point (h_2 on Figure 25) depends on the height of the water table above sea level (h_1).

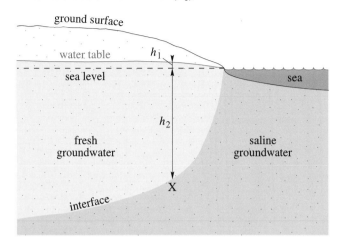

Figure 22 A cross-section illustrating the relationship between fresh groundwater and saline groundwater at a coast. The vertical scale is exaggerated. The depth of the saline water below sea level (h_2) is about forty times the height of the water table above sea level (h_1).

Along this interface the pressures due to the head of denser saline water and the less dense fresh water must balance. Earlier we defined the head of water simply as the difference in height (and therefore in pressure) between two points. Here we are dealing with waters of different density, for saline water is denser than fresh water. So, if we wish to compare pressure differences caused by the different heads of saline water and fresh water we have to introduce density into the calculations. At any point on the interface (X on Figure 22) the pressure due to the saline water will be given by the depth of that point below sea level (i.e. the head of saline water, h_2), multiplied by the density of the saline water (ρ_s). At the same point on the interface the pressure caused by the fresh groundwater will be given by the depth of the point below the water table (i.e. the head of fresh water, $h_1 + h_2$, multiplied by the density of the fresh water, ρ_f). These pressures must balance at point X:

$$h_2\rho_s = (h_1 + h_2)\rho_f$$

or by rearranging the equation,

$$h_2 = \frac{\rho_f}{\rho_s - \rho_f} h_1 \tag{3.4}$$

As $\rho_f = 10^3 \, \text{kg m}^{-3}$ and ρ_s is typically $1.025 \times 10^3 \, \text{kg m}^{-3}$,

$$h_2 = \frac{10^3}{(1.025 - 1) \times 10^3} h_1$$

$$h_2 = 40h_1 \tag{3.5}$$

This means that if the water table near a coast is, say, 5 m above sea level (that is, $h_1 = 5$ m), then

$$h_1 + h_2 = 5 + (40 \times 5) = 205 \text{ m}$$

and therefore saline groundwater should be found at a depth of 205 m below the water table. Also, a drawdown of 1 m in a well would produce a rise of 40 m in the saline water below the well.

Activity 4

Sketch the new position of the water table and the interface of fresh groundwater and saline groundwater onto Figure 22, corresponding to a well drawdown above point X of 1 m, with h_1 as 5 m. Start by using Equation 3.5 to calculate h_2 before and during pumping.

If the densities of the fresh or saline water vary, so will the $40:1$ ratio of h_2 to h_1. This would occur where brackish waters form the interface with fresh water. However, the interface between fresh groundwater and saline groundwater is usually not as sharp as is implied in Figure 22. Instead there is normally a zone, at least a few metres in width, where the fresh and saline groundwaters mix. The water in this zone is less saline than seawater; that is, it is brackish water. The level of the sea rises and falls with the tides, and there are variations in the rate of discharge of fresh groundwater to the sea. These factors bring about changes in the position of the interface, and can promote mixing of fresh water and seawater. Figure 23 shows a zone of mixing between 200 m and 500 m wide off the coast of Florida.

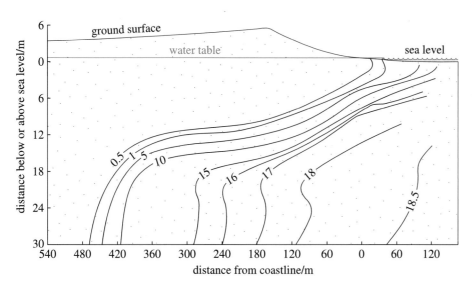

Figure 23 Mixing at the fresh groundwater/saline groundwater interface at Biscayne Bay, Florida. The contour values are chloride concentrations in grams per litre. The 18.5 g l⁻¹ contour represents seawater, and the 0.5 g l⁻¹ contour fresh water. Intermediate values result from the mixing of seawater and fresh water.

Seawater intrusion into wells can become a problem where large amounts of groundwater are pumped from the ground near a coast. Under natural conditions fresh groundwater discharges to the sea, but if too much groundwater is abstracted near a coast, saline groundwater moves inland. This is called a **saline intrusion**. If the water table is lowered by high rates of abstraction (h_1 is reduced), the position of the interface between the fresh and saline groundwater rises (h_2 is reduced), so the wells may eventually be filled with saline water and become useless for supplying fresh water. These problems can become acute on small islands, where there is usually a lens-shaped body of fresh groundwater overlying saline groundwater, which is in contact with seawater around the island (Figure 24).

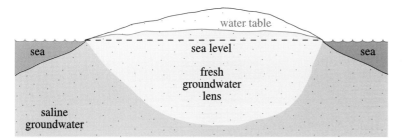

Figure 24 Fresh groundwater and saline groundwater below an island. A lens-shaped body of fresh water occurs below the island.

Saline intrusions along coasts can be controlled by limiting the rate at which groundwater is removed so that the water table remains above sea level and slopes down towards the coast. Providing the hydraulic gradient is seawards, fresh groundwater will flow in this direction, preventing further saline intrusion. This method of control is practised in eastern England. Saline intrusion can also be controlled by injecting fresh water into the ground. This can be either surplus water collected during wet months or water of low quality which would otherwise be discharged into the sea. The water is

Saline intrusion at Dakar

Dakar is the capital of the western African state of Senegal. It lies on a cape that juts out into the Atlantic Ocean, originally called Cap Vert (Green Cape) because of its once abundant vegetation, although it is now dry, desolate and no longer green.

Most (80%) of the water supply to the 1.5 million people in Dakar comes from groundwater, pumped from local wells. The rest is expensively brought from a lake 300 km away. Water consumption has increased with population growth and industrialization in Dakar, causing more water to be pumped from the wells. The water table has fallen and the level of saline water has risen, contaminating some of the wells. It is predicted that if pumping continues at the present rate, all of Dakar's wells will be contaminated with saline water in about fifty years.

To prevent this, Dakar will have to either (a) reduce its water consumption, (b) manage pumping by adjusting pumping rates from different wells, without reducing the total output, to allow some of the fresh water to flow towards the sea and hold back the seawater, or (c) bring extra surface water from the lake through a canal. All three options are being attempted.

injected into the ground by secondary wells situated between the main extraction wells and the coast. Sewage effluent is used to control saline intrusions by this method on the western coast of the United States and in Israel.

3.5 Porosity

The amount of water that a rock can store depends on its porosity, which is the proportion of the volume of the rock that consists of pores:

$$\text{porosity (\%)} = \frac{\text{pore volume}}{\text{total volume}} \times 100 \qquad (3.6)$$

The principal factors that control porosity are grain size and shape, the degree of sorting, the extent of cementing of grains and the amount of fracturing. Figure 25 illustrates how porosity varies with the degree of sorting and with the grain shape in unconsolidated sediments (sediments that have not been compacted or cemented).

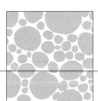

(a) high porosity: rounded grains, uniform size (good sorting)

(b) low porosity: rounded grains, many sizes (poor sorting)

(c) medium porosity: angular grains, uniform size (good sorting)

(d) very low porosity: angular grains, many sizes (poor sorting)

Figure 25 Porosity in unconsolidated sediments varies with the degree of sorting and with the shape of the grains. Each illustration shows an area 1 cm across.

Question 13

(a) Why do examples (a) and (c) in Figure 25 represent well-sorted sediments, and (b) and (d) represent poorly sorted sediments?

(b) Which are more porous — well-sorted sediments or poorly sorted sediments?

(c) Given similar degrees of sorting, how does porosity vary with the roundness of the grains?

(d) Estimate the porosity of the sediments (a) to (d), selecting a value from the following ranges for each: less than 10%; 10–20%; 20–30%; 30–40%.

Unconsolidated sediments with rounded grains of uniform size (i.e. ideally sorted) are the most porous. Sediments decrease in porosity as the angularity of the grains increases because the grains can pack more closely together, the bumps of some grains fitting into indentations in others (Figure 25, examples c and d). There is also lower porosity if the sediment is poorly sorted, because small grains can occupy the spaces between larger grains.

Consolidated (compacted and/or cemented) sedimentary rocks, and igneous and metamorphic rocks are usually less porous than unconsolidated sediments (Table 5). The cement in consolidated sedimentary rocks occupies what would otherwise be spaces between the grains, so a sandstone, for example, will be less porous than a sand with grains of similar size. Igneous and metamorphic rocks generally have very low porosity, because crystals interlock in them. However, there are volcanic rocks that contain gas bubbles (Figure 26a) and some of these have quite high porosities.

Table 5 Porosities and hydraulic conductivities

Geological material	Grain size/mm	Porosity (%)	Hydraulic conductivity/m per day
Unconsolidated sediments			
clay	0.000 5 to 0.002	45 to 60	less than 10^{-2}
silt	0.002 to 0.06	40 to 50	10^{-2} to 1
sand	0.06 to 2	30 to 40	1 to 5×10^2
gravel	2 to 64	25 to 35	5×10^2 to 1×10^4
Consolidated sedimentary rocks			
shale	small	5 to 15	5×10^{-8} to 5×10^{-6}
sandstone	medium	5 to 30	10^{-4} to 10 *
limestone	variable	10^{-1} to 30 (secondary porosity)	10^{-5} to 10 *
Igneous and metamorphic rocks			
basalt	small	10^{-3} to 1 (up to 50 if vesicular)	3×10^{-4} to 3*
granite	large	10^{-4} to 1 (up to 10 if fractured)	3×10^{-4} to 1*
slate	small	10^{-3} to 1	10^{-8} to 10^{-5}
schist	medium	10^{-3} to 1	10^{-7} to 10^{-1}

* Values at the higher end of the range occur where there is secondary permeability.

The porosity of rocks may be increased by processes that occur *after* the rocks have formed. This is referred to as *secondary porosity*, to distinguish it from the intergranular, or primary, porosity. One type of secondary porosity is fracture porosity, caused by cracks in rocks (Figure 26b). Another type of secondary porosity is solution porosity, which develops where part of a rock has been dissolved, leaving open spaces (Figure 26c). This is common in limestones, which are dissolved by acidic rainwater and groundwater, and immense caverns may be formed by this process.

(a) vesicular porosity: may not be interconnected e.g. basalt

(b) porosity along fractures or bedding planes e.g. sandstone

(c) solution porosity e.g. limestone

Figure 26 Porosity in consolidated rocks. Example (b) shows bedding planes rather than individual grains, so covers a much larger area of rock: (a) and (c) are 1 cm across, but (b) is 10 m across.

3.6 Permeability

It is important to distinguish clearly between porosity and permeability. Porosity is a measure of *how much* water can be stored in a rock, whereas permeability is a measure of the properties of a rock which determine *how fast* water can *flow* through it. Permeability depends on the extent to which pores are *interconnected*.

Table 5 gives the porosity and hydraulic conductivity of various rocks. As hydraulic conductivity depends on permeability, the values in the last column could be said to represent relative permeabilities. However, hydraulic conductivities rather than permeabilities are given in the Table, because these can be used to calculate flow rates using Darcy's law (Equation 3.1).

For unconsolidated sediments, the coarser sands and gravels are more permeable than the finer grained silts and clays, even though they are less porous (Table 5). There are two major reasons for this: first, the smaller grain sizes in silt and clay result in a greater surface area of particles relative to volume, so water tends to be held in the pores by surface tension; and second, the platy and angular shape of clay particles means that they tend to interlock and isolate the spaces between them, which further inhibits the movement of water through the sediment.

Which four of the sediments and rocks in Figures 25 and 26 should have the highest permeabilities and which two should have the lowest permeabilities?

Rocks that are highly permeable must have interconnected pores; so Figure 25, examples (a) and (c), and Figure 26, examples (b) and (c), should have high permeabilities (even though Figure 26, example (b), has a low *porosity*). Rocks with a low permeability must have isolated pores, so the water cannot move through the rock, and Figure 25, example (d), and Figure 26, example (a), should have low permeabilities.

Usually, consolidated and cemented sedimentary rocks (and igneous and metamorphic rocks) are not very permeable; but sometimes *secondary permeability*, caused by processes such as solution or fracturing, increases the overall permeability. The higher hydraulic conductivities of some of the igneous, metamorphic and consolidated sedimentary rocks in Table 5 are mainly due to secondary permeability caused by fracturing.

3.7 Aquifers

A layer of rock that is sufficiently porous to store water, and permeable enough to allow water to flow through it, is called an **aquifer**. Aquifers are introduced on p. 32 of *The Geological Map* booklet.

The best aquifers are unconsolidated sands and gravels because they are relatively porous and very permeable. Consolidated rocks, for example, sandstone and limestone, can also form important and extensive aquifers.

Although the porosity of an aquifer is a measure of the amount of water stored within the pores or fissures, it does not provide a direct measure of the amount of water that may be *recovered* by pumping or drainage. This is because a proportion of the water is always retained around the individual grains by surface tension, and this is known as the **specific retention**.

The **specific yield** is the maximum amount of water that can be recovered. Figure 27 illustrates the relationship between specific yield and porosity, which is expressed by the equation:

specific yield = porosity − specific retention   (3.7)

All three terms in the equation are expressed as *percentages* of the total volume of the rock. The specific retention decreases with increasing grain size in unconsolidated sediments (Figure 27). (A few large particles would have a smaller total surface area than a lot of smaller particles occupying the same volume, and a smaller surface area retains less water by surface tension.) This means that less water is retained in coarse-grained sediments. However, the specific yield is greatest for medium-grained sediments (sands), rather than for coarse-grained sediments, because the porosity decreases with increasing grain size.

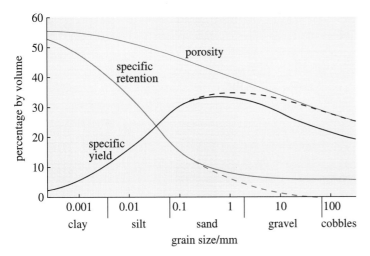

Figure 27 Relationship between porosity, specific yield, specific retention and grain size, for unconsolidated sediments only. The broken lines give values for well-sorted aquifers. The grain size is logarithmic. The lines on this graph are best-fit curves drawn through scattered points; you should not ascribe any degree of precision to them.

The **exploitable storage** of water in an aquifer is the *volume* of water it will yield:

$$\text{exploitable storage} = V \times \frac{Y}{100}$$ (3.8)

where V is the volume of the aquifer that is being exploited, and Y the specific yield. It is important to distinguish between the specific yield (a percentage of the volume of the rock) and the exploitable storage (a volume of water).

Question 14

Pumping from an unconsolidated aquifer lowered the water table by an average of 5 m over an area of $8 \times 10^5 \text{ m}^2$.

(a) If the porosity of the aquifer averages 37% and the specific retention is 7%, calculate the specific yield of the rock.

(b) From this value, calculate the volume of water that was actually removed.

(c) From Figure 27, what type of material is indicated by the data in (a)?

There are two types of aquifer, unconfined and confined, distinguished on the basis of their geological structure in relation to the position of the saturated zone.

1   **Unconfined aquifers**   These outcrop at the ground surface. The water table is the top of the saturated zone in an unconfined aquifer, and water normally has to be pumped to the surface except where the water table actually intersects the surface of the ground and forms a spring. A thin impermeable layer sometimes occurs locally in an aquifer, and this may support a small **perched aquifer**, separated from the main water table (see Figure 28).

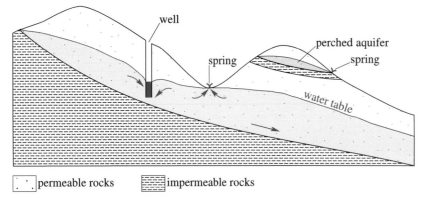

permeable rocks   impermeable rocks

Figure 28   Unconfined and perched aquifers. Water discharges at the springs. Water extracted from the well causes drawdown into a cone of depression in the water table around the well. The arrows show the directions in which groundwater flows. Water is not shown in the impermeable rock below the aquifer because although it is in the saturated zone, the water moves too slowly to be economically recoverable.

2   **Confined aquifers**   These are separated from the ground surface by an impermeable layer (right-hand side of Figure 29) and are generally at greater depths than unconfined aquifers. Pressures in confined aquifers may be sufficient for the water in wells that penetrate the aquifer to discharge naturally at the surface without pumping (the right-hand well in Figure 29).

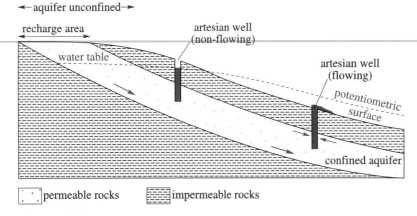

permeable rocks   impermeable rocks

Figure 29   A confined aquifer. The arrows show the directions of groundwater flow. To the left of the diagram the aquifer outcrops and so is unconfined; the aquifer is recharged in this area. The unconfined area extends to the intersection of the water table with the overlying impermeable rock. Here the potentiometric surface is also the water table.

Water in confined aquifers is called artesian water and a well that penetrates a confined aquifer is called an **artesian well**. The height to which water will rise in a well is called the potentiometric level and the **potentiometric surface** is an imaginary surface joining the potentiometric levels for a confined aquifer. For an unconfined aquifer, the potentiometric surface is the water table. The gradient of the potentiometric surface in a confined aquifer can be used to calculate groundwater flow rates, just as the water table gradients are used to work out flow rates in unconfined aquifers using Darcy's law (Equation 3.1). The potentiometric surface is usually curved, because the pressure required to overcome friction, as water moves through pores in the rocks, results in a decrease in the pressure head. Even if the pressure head is insufficient for water to rise to the surface, water in artesian wells rises above the top of the aquifer at the point where the well lies.

For artesian pressure to be maintained, the water that flows from the well must be replaced by water that infiltrates into the aquifer where it outcrops and is thus unconfined (that is, the same aquifer can be confined in one area and unconfined in another — see the right-hand and left-hand sides of Figure 29). This area of outcrop is called the **recharge area** of the aquifer. Like wells in unconfined aquifers, non-flowing artesian wells (the left-hand well in Figure 29) have a cone of depression when they are pumped.

Naturally flowing artesian springs occur where the potentiometric surface is above the ground surface. An **oasis** in the desert is a natural artesian spring, where groundwater is being discharged to the surface. Oases can occur where the crest of a fold in a confined aquifer is intersected by the ground surface, or where water can rise to the surface along a fault where the potentiometric surface is above ground level (Figure 30). The water discharged at oases is often recharged in mountainous areas, which may be at a great distance from the oasis. This suggests that the groundwater in large, confined aquifers may be of considerable age; i.e. much time has elapsed since the water fell as rain. An example is the Nubian sandstone, which is a confined aquifer in the form of a broad fold that underlies a large part of northern Africa. Artesian water in the Nubian sandstone aquifer has been dated using carbon isotopes, giving ages of up to 40 000 years. Such dates make it possible to calculate groundwater speeds and, from Darcy's law, the hydraulic conductivity of the aquifer.

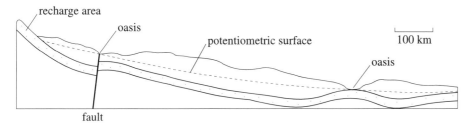

Figure 30 A confined aquifer can give rise to oases in desert regions, either by seepage up fault planes or by actual exposure of the aquifer at the surface due to folding.

In Figure 30 the artesian water at the oasis that is furthest from the recharge area was dated as 40 000 years old. What is the average speed at which groundwater flows through the aquifer, in metres per day?

The oasis is about 900 km from the recharge area, so

$$\text{speed of flow} = \frac{\text{distance}}{\text{age (time taken)}}$$

$$= \frac{900}{40\,000} \text{ km per year}$$

$$= 0.02 \text{ km per year}$$

which is about 0.06 m per day.

The fall and rise of groundwater under London

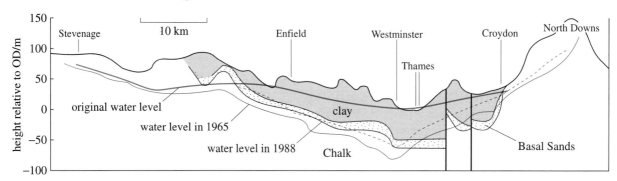

Figure 31 A geological cross-section through London. The section runs north–south, with north to the left of the figure. There is a large vertical exaggeration on this section (see vertical and horizontal scales). 'OD' on the vertical scale refers to a level, 'ordnance datum' (roughly sea level) so that positive values are heights above this, and negative values depths below. The Chalk and Basal Sands are a confined aquifer, beneath the impermeable clay layers. The vertical black lines to the south of the Thames are faults. The original water level in the aquifer (the potentiometric surface) is given by the blue line.

London is underlain by a confined aquifer, the Chalk, which is a limestone of Cretaceous age, and the overlying Basal Sands, of Tertiary age. (These form part of the Cretaceous and Tertiary sequences on the *Postcard Geological Map*.) The aquifer is folded, with the deepest part below central London (Figure 31; see also p. 25 and p. 26 of *The Geological Map* booklet), and is overlain by Tertiary sediments that are mainly clays. This aquifer is recharged on the Chalk outcrops in the Chiltern Hills, Berkshire Downs and North Downs. Under natural conditions, groundwater flowed through the confined aquifer and discharged into the Thames Valley.

During the nineteenth and twentieth centuries water has been pumped from the aquifer for the public water supply, industrial and commercial uses. Water levels in the aquifer had fallen by up to 70 m in the mid-1960s. The fall in the potentiometric surface:

- stopped the natural discharge to the River Thames below London;
- led to saline intrusion from the River Thames below London;
- reduced the flow of springs from the outcrop and reduced river flows;

- increased the rate of flow of groundwater through the confined aquifer, because of the steeper hydraulic gradient;
- allowed water to drain from the clays overlying the confined aquifer and as a result the ground surface subsided by up to several tens of centimetres.

Some of these may seem to be undesirable consequences but this was offset by the ready availability of groundwater below London during the nineteenth and twentieth centuries, which played an important role in the economic development of the city.

As London expanded, higher buildings with deep basements and foundations were constructed. Also, expansion of the public transport system and other services led to the construction of deep tunnels to avoid using surface land. These foundations and tunnels were designed for the low groundwater levels and clay properties at that time.

Since the mid-1960s less groundwater has been taken from wells in London. This has led to a steady rise in groundwater levels (Figure 32). The reduction is attributed to: industrial decentralization from London, the introduction of licensing

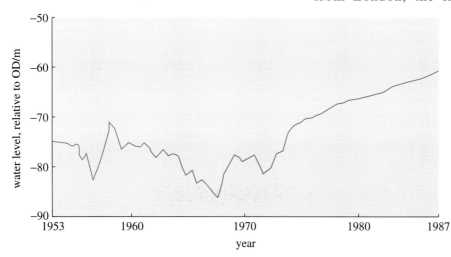

Figure 32 The water level in a well at Trafalgar Square, 1953–87. In 1850 the level was about −22 m OD, falling gradually to about −80 m OD in 1950. Since 1974 the rise has been fairly uniform at 0.8 m per year.

controls on private extractions, and the high cost of pumping.

There is concern that if groundwater levels continue to rise, underground structures in London could be endangered by flooding of basements and tunnels, increased water pressures, swelling of clay and chemical attack on buried concrete and steel — an environmental problem for the future.

Because groundwater flows so slowly, the water in large artesian aquifers is not always renewed as fast as it is extracted. Also, the water may have been precipitated when the climate was very different: the oldest Nubian artesian water, for example, fell as rain at a time when the climate was cooler and wetter. Since then the area has become much warmer and drier, so the aquifer is recharging much more slowly. Under such circumstances, water in some large artesian aquifers in semi-arid regions is in practice a *non-renewable resource*.

All the same, in the *short* term, it is possible to increase the amount of water being taken from an aquifer and to 'mine' water (which will be replaced very slowly or not at all), because the volume of water stored in an aquifer is usually large compared with the amount being removed. In the longer term, however, mining water will have adverse effects, including a lowered water table, a need for more expensive pumping from greater depths, a reduced flow to springs and rivers, and possibly a deterioration in water quality.

In general, the rate at which water is removed from an aquifer should not reduce the average water table level or have other adverse effects. The maximum quantity of water that can be safely removed from an aquifer annually is termed the **safe yield** for the aquifer.

3.8 Exploration for groundwater

Although groundwater is not visible, there are methods that can be employed to locate it from the surface. Such methods are often used in the initial reconnaissance, because they work out much cheaper than sinking boreholes in search of water.

3.8.1 Geological methods

The first step is to study the surface geology, using any geological maps that are available, in order to map the different rock types at the surface. Once the porosity and permeability of these rocks have been determined, possible aquifers can be identified and it may be possible to predict their subsurface size and shape.

In the UK, geological maps are readily available, but in many countries they do not exist, or exist for only parts of the country. Here, aerial photographs may be useful. They show drainage patterns, and it may be possible to identify springs or seepages of groundwater at the surface. Remote sensing (for example, with satellite images) can also be useful, to indicate changes in the land-surface characteristics, such as seasonal changes in vegetation that relate to the availability of groundwater.

In order to evaluate the amount of groundwater present, it is important to understand the geological structure of the area. Folds influence the direction in which groundwater flows (water often, although not always, tends to move down the dip in inclined strata; Figure 29) and they can bring water in a confined aquifer to the surface (Figure 30). Faults may do the same, or may form subsurface barriers against the flow of water. Fractured and fissured rocks near or within a fault zone can also increase both the secondary porosity and the secondary permeability of rocks in the area, and in some places major fault zones can be important aquifers.

If there are no suitable sedimentary rock aquifers, groundwater must be sought in zones of secondary permeability in igneous and metamorphic rocks.

3.8.2 Hydrological methods

Hydrological methods of groundwater exploration include investigations of the water available for recharging the aquifer — from precipitation and surface water — and the location and quantity of groundwater discharged at the surface. The rate of infiltration is also important: if the surface rocks are impermeable, water will run off them rapidly and there will be little infiltration and recharge. The location and distribution of springs can also be used to map the position of the potentiometric surface, and may indicate the existence of impermeable rocks (Figure 20b).

3.8.3 Geophysical methods

If these geological and hydrological studies have not provided enough information, the subsurface structure can be further investigated by using geophysical methods, which detect and measure the variations in physical properties *below* the Earth's surface. Geophysical studies cannot determine the presence of water or the porosity or permeability of a rock directly, but can be used to determine the structure of rocks under the surface and the possible location of a water table. They may also identify other rock properties that can give an indication of whether a rock formation is an aquifer, and if so what its volume and extent may be.

The most widely used geophysical technique for groundwater exploration is the measurement of **resistivity** (see Box below).

The Box 'The water supply near Shugborough Park' illustrates a groundwater exploration problem that was solved by a horizontal profiling resistivity survey.

The Box 'The aquifer near Stone' illustrates the results of vertical sounding resistivity surveys that were made to determine the extent of an aquifer in Staffordshire, using the difference in the resistivities of different rock types.

Resistivity surveys

The resistivity of a rock is a measure of the resistance of the rock to the flow of an electrical current through it. It has the unit of ohm-metres. The lower the resistivity, the easier it is for current to flow. The resistivity of most rocks is controlled mainly by the water content and the salinity, and not by the rock type, except where the rocks contain ore minerals. The passage of electric currents in rocks takes place through conduction by ions in the groundwater. The resistivity of dry rocks is higher than that of water-containing rocks, because resistivity is the inverse of conductivity. An increase in the concentration of ions in the water, measured by the salinity, leads to a corresponding decrease in resistivity. Thus, (a) wet rocks, or rocks below the water table, have lower resistivities than those above the water table, and (b) groundwater with a high salinity has a lower resistivity than fresh water.

Resistivity surveys are made by introducing an electric current into the ground between two metal electrodes connected to a battery. The current travels not only in a straight line between the electrodes but also down into the underlying rocks. The resistivity of the rock is measured by another pair of electrodes in the ground, which detect the current.

If the electrodes are moved along the surface, the horizontal variation of subsurface resistivity can be measured. This is the *horizontal profiling* resistivity technique.

It is also possible to use resistivity to determine how rocks change with depth, in the *vertical sounding* technique. For this, the electrodes are kept centred on one spot, while the spacing between them is increased. The second pair of electrodes then records current (and therefore resistivity) that has travelled to greater depths.

The water supply near Shugborough Park, Staffordshire

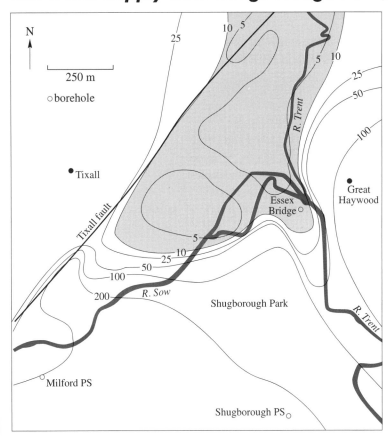

The Shugborough Park area of Staffordshire is underlain by Triassic sandstones, a consolidated aquifer, covered by the sands and gravels of the Trent River Valley. Three wells had been drilled into the sandstones for water supplies, and two of these, at Milford and Shugborough, supply fresh water, whereas the well at Essex Bridge produced unusable highly saline water. Before any new wells could be drilled, it was necessary to determine the extent of the saline water in the area in order to avoid it. This could have been located by drilling exploration boreholes, but it was cheaper to make a horizontal profiling resistivity survey of the area. Figure 33 shows the results in terms of the resistivity of the sandstone bedrock. The location of the highly saline groundwater was recognized from the low resistivity values between the Tixall Fault and Essex Bridge.

Figure 33 Map of bedrock resistivity near Shugborough Park, Staffordshire. Contours are in ohm-metres. The presence of strongly saline groundwater is indicated by resistivities below 10 ohm-metres (the grey area). The Milford and Shugborough pumping stations supply fresh water, but the Essex Bridge well produced very saline water. PS, pumping station.

The aquifer near Stone, Staffordshire

The aquifer is Triassic sandstone, and three wells were planned in the area to extract water from it. The aquifer is unconfined in this area, but its structure was unknown. The only information available was that it is underlain by relatively impermeable Carboniferous marl (a calcareous mudstone). The large difference in resistivity between the marl (measured from surface outcrops as 76 ohm-metres) and the overlying sandstone (600 ohm-metres) indicated that the resistivity technique should be suitable for exploring the area. The results of vertical

sounding resistivity surveys, and the geology inferred from them, are shown in Figure 34. These results reveal that the aquifer is not continuous, but is divided into a number of smaller isolated units by upfaulted blocks of the impermeable marl. The data were used together with other resistivity results to determine the location of the pumping stations and to make estimates of the volume and safe yield of the aquifer. Rates of extraction were calculated so that wells of the right size could be drilled, and pumps of adequate power installed.

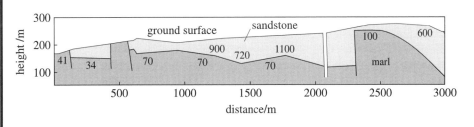

Figure 34 Resistivity values, in ohm-metres, and deduced geology in a cross-section of an area near Stone, Staffordshire. The sandstone is an important aquifer.

Other geophysical techniques used for groundwater exploration include gravity surveys and seismic techniques. These are used much less often than resistivity, but may be useful to determine the structure of an area. These techniques are discussed in Block 4 *Energy 1 – Fossil Fuels*.

3.8.4 Boreholes

The most direct (but most expensive) method of exploring for groundwater is by drilling boreholes. Samples of the subsurface rock ('chippings') are brought back to the surface during drilling, or the well can be 'logged', by making geophysical measurements of the surrounding rocks down the borehole (this is also discussed in more detail in Block 4 *Energy 1*), or, even more expensively, core can be drilled and returned to the surface. Boreholes are essential for relating the subsurface physical properties obtained from geophysical surveys to the rocks themselves — for example, porosity and permeability can be measured in a laboratory from core samples.

3.9 Summary of Section 3

1   The rate at which water infiltrates into the ground depends on the permeability of the rocks and the state of the ground surface. Below the ground surface there is an aeration zone which has air in pore spaces, and a saturated zone which has all the pores filled with water. The water table is the boundary between the aeration zone and the saturated zone, and is the level at which water stands in wells. Water below the water table is called groundwater. The water table follows the topography of the ground surface but with more gentle gradients.

2   Groundwater will flow in response to differences in pressure. Darcy's law relates the speed of the groundwater movement (v) to the hydraulic conductivity (K) and to the hydraulic gradient or slope of the water table (h/l) by:

$$v = K \frac{h}{l}$$

The hydraulic conductivity depends on the permeability of the rock and on properties of the water. Water will flow in the direction of maximum slope of the water table.

3   A cone of depression is formed in the water level around a well from which water is being pumped. The difference in height between the water table before pumping and the water level in the well during pumping is called the drawdown.

4   There is usually saline groundwater under the land at a coast, with a wedge of saline groundwater under the fresh groundwater. The depth of the saline groundwater depends on the height of the water table above sea level and on the densities of the fresh and saline water.

5   The porosity of a rock is the proportion of the volume of the rock that consists of pores:

$$\text{porosity (\%)} = \frac{\text{pore volume}}{\text{total volume}} \times 100$$

Porosity is a measure of how much water a rock can store. The permeability of a rock is a measure of the properties of the rock which determine how fast water can flow through it. The porosity and permeability are generally greater in unconsolidated sedimentary rocks, particularly sands and gravels, than in consolidated sedimentary, igneous or metamorphic rocks. Both porosity and permeability can be increased by processes that occur after the formation of the rock, such as solution or fracturing. This is called secondary porosity and secondary permeability.

6   An aquifer is a rock that can store water, and through which water can flow. For a rock to be an aquifer it must be sufficiently porous and it must be permeable. The best aquifers are sands and gravels. Igneous and metamorphic rocks seldom make good aquifers unless they have secondary porosity and secondary permeability.

7   The amount of water that can be recovered from a saturated aquifer is known as the specific yield. This is less than the total amount of water in the aquifer (represented by the porosity) because part of the water is retained by surface tension around the individual grains. Specific yield, like porosity, is expressed as a percentage of the total volume of the rock. The highest porosities are found in fine-grained sediments, but the greatest specific yields are in medium-grained sediments. The exploitable storage of a saturated aquifer is the volume of water it will give up when pumped or allowed to drain.

8   Aquifers can be unconfined or confined. Unconfined aquifers outcrop at the ground surface; water normally has to be pumped to the surface from these aquifers. Confined aquifers are separated from the ground surface by an impermeable layer. Water in confined aquifers is is called artesian water, and wells that penetrate into confined aquifers are called artesian wells. The water in an artesian well may be under sufficient pressure to reach the surface of the ground without pumping (a flowing artesian well).

9   The potentiometric surface is an imaginary surface joining the height to which water will rise in wells. For an unconfined aquifer, the potentiometric surface is the water table.

10   The safe yield of an aquifer is the maximum rate of abstraction of water that does not produce a long-term decline in the average water table level or have any other adverse effect, such as a significant reduction in the flow to springs and rivers. Exceeding the safe yield would necessitate pumping from greater depths to obtain water, and might lead to a deterioration in water quality.

11   Exploration for groundwater involves a combination of geological, hydrological, geophysical and borehole techniques.

Question 15

Calculate the hydraulic conductivity of the aquifer in Figure 30. The average difference in height between the recharge area and the furthest oasis is 2000 m, and the speed of flow (as calculated in Section 3.7) is about 0.06 m per day.

Question 16

In broad terms, how does porosity vary with the grain size of (a) unconsolidated sediments and (b) consolidated sediments?

Question 17

Match the items 1 to 9 with the letters A to I on Figure 35. Each item and letter should be used only once.

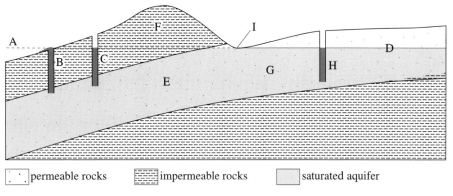

| permeable rocks | impermeable rocks | saturated aquifer |

1 aeration zone
2 unconfined aquifer
3 confined aquifer
4 water table
5 potentiometric surface
6 well in unconfined aquifer
7 flowing artesian well
8 non-flowing artesian well
9 spring

Figure 35

Activity 5

Some of the important aquifers in the south-western USA are the sediments that fill enclosed valleys or basins between the mountains. The sediments are unconsolidated silts, sands and gravels that have been eroded from the mountains by heavy, seasonal rainstorms and deposited by floods in the valleys below. One such aquifer is shown in plan view in Figure 36. The sediments are completely surrounded by and underlain by impermeable bedrock. The sediments are up to 50 m in thickness in the centre of the basin and thin out at the edges. The upper surface of the sediments slopes gently downwards to the north-east but in a north-west to south-east direction the surface can be considered flat.

After winter rainstorms a river flows across the aquifer from the south-west and recharges the aquifer. Contours of the height of the water table relative to a reference datum are shown on Figure 36 for the situation that exists soon after the end of the dry season.

Draw the directions of groundwater flow onto Figure 36. Draw enough flow lines to show how groundwater flows throughout the whole aquifer.

Figure 36 Water-table contour map for a basin aquifer in the south-western United States, for use with Activities 5 and 6. The points A, B and C are not used in Activity 5 but will be used in Activity 6.

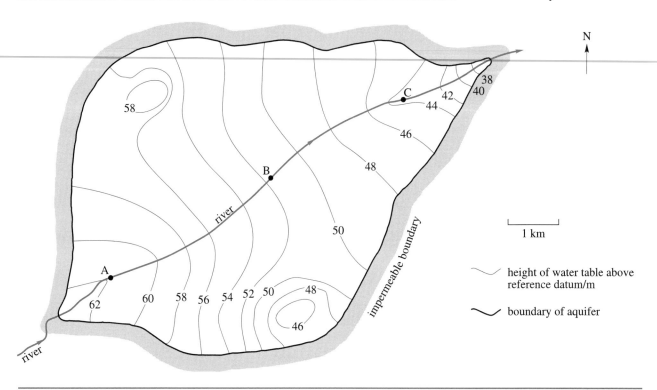

4 SURFACE WATER

4.1 Springs

We have seen that where precipitation reaches the ground, some of it infiltrates and the rest runs off the surface into streams and rivers. However, the water that infiltrates to become groundwater may eventually re-emerge at the surface as springs where the water table intersects the surface. Indeed, many streams and rivers have springs as their ultimate source, or are fed by them at various points along their courses.

In Section 3.7 we looked at the artesian springs that are associated with confined aquifers. These are most obvious on land, but can also occur on the sea bed, a fact long known to sailors who have used them to fill up with fresh water while still at sea. In such cases, a confined aquifer has its recharge area on land but extends beyond the coast to underlie the sea bed, and if the geology and topography are favourable, the aquifer intersects the sea bed some distance from shore, thus allowing fresh water to emerge at the sea bed.

Most springs, however, are ordinary water-table springs, and these can be of several different kinds depending on the geological setting:

1   *Valley springs* develop in valleys where the surface of the ground intersects the water table (Figures 16c and 28). In southern England, a number of seasonal valley springs occur in the Chalk when the water table rises during a wet winter. These temporary streams are called bournes, reflected in some of the place names in the area, e.g. Winterbourne Stoke in Dorset. These bournes dry up in summer, when the water table drops below the ground surface.

2   *Stratum springs* form where the downward flow of groundwater is prevented by an underlying impermeable layer of rock, which can result in a line of springs emerging at the boundary between the two layers (Figure 20b).

3   *Solution channel springs* typically occur in limestone districts where groundwater has created underground caves and channels by dissolving calcium carbonate along bedding planes and fractures, and then returned to the surface where impermeable strata prevent further downwards migration.

4.2 River flow

The water in a river comes not only from overland flow, precipitation and springs, but also from the underground flow of water to the river. The river can receive water from **throughflow**, which is that part of infiltration that moves through the aeration zone without penetrating to the main water table. It occurs because the permeability of the aeration zone tends to reduce with depth thereby restricting infiltration. The term includes water that flows from any perched water tables in the aeration zone.

Groundwater that discharges to a river is called **base flow** (Figure 37). The contribution of the base flow to the river flow varies greatly with the geology and topography of the area and with the season. The base-flow contribution is low for a river in a catchment area of impermeable rocks, where rainfall infiltrates only slowly, and the overland flow is consequently high. In contrast, for rivers with catchments of permeable rocks there may be no **surface runoff** in the rivers (the part of the river flow which comes from overland flow), with most of the rainfall infiltrating into the ground. Most of the river flow in this case will be base flow. In Britain, the base flow usually forms a higher proportion of the total flow in summer than in winter, because evaporation is higher in summer and surface runoff is therefore lower, whereas the water stored in the permeable rocks is released to rivers as base flow more consistently throughout the year.

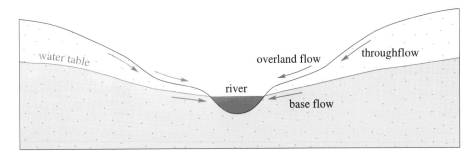

Figure 37 The discharge of a river comes from overland flow, throughflow and groundwater base flow. Arrows show the direction of flow.

The **discharge** of a river is the volume of water that flows past a point in a certain time. The measurement, or gauging, of river discharge is necessary for the calculation of surface water resources. Discharge values also give information about the maximum and minimum volumes of water flowing in the river, which is required for water supply schemes and for flood-control and hydroelectric projects. The discharge (Q) of a river is related to the speed of flow (v) by the equation:

$$Q = Av \tag{4.1}$$

where A is the cross-sectional area. This equation is identical to Equation 3.2 for groundwater flow.

The cross-sectional area of a river channel at some point is determined from measurements of the depth of the water taken at known intervals across the river. The speed of the flow can be measured using current meters; these have vanes that are turned by the water flowing past, the rate of rotation giving the water speed. The speed is not constant from bank to bank or from the bed to the surface, however, so a number of speed measurements must be made at different depths at intervals across the river. The river cross-section is divided into small areas, and the discharge within each area is calculated (area × speed across that section). The total discharge is the sum of the individual discharges.

This method is very laborious, as many speed–depth measurements have to be made for each determination of discharge. However, once the discharge at a particular water level has been measured, the assumption is made that if the water level in the river at that point (the **stage**) is the same, the discharge will be the same. This means that if the discharge in the river has been measured at different stages, so that the relationship between stage and discharge is known, the river discharge can be estimated from measurement of stage alone; this is read directly from a post in the river. Figure 38 shows a **rating curve** for a river; it is a plot of discharge values measured at various stages, with a smooth curve drawn through the plotted points. The shapes of rating curves can vary considerably: they do not have to be similar to the curve in Figure 38.

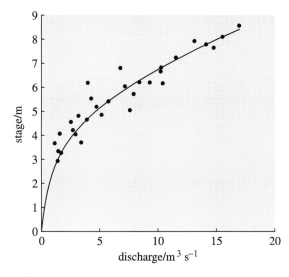

Figure 38 A river rating curve. A best-fit line is drawn through the measured values.

How accurately do you think the discharge can be estimated from the stage, using a rating curve?

Not very accurately, because there is a scatter of measured points about the curve. The assumption that discharge and stage are related is only approximately correct, as the discharge for a given stage will vary slightly depending on whether the river level is static, rising or falling, and on whether the cross-sectional area of the river has changed on account of erosion or the deposition of sediment on the river bed. Where possible, concrete weirs, which have a horizontal surface and a constant cross-sectional area, are built into the river at gauging stations to reduce the errors involved in using rating curves to estimate discharge.

A record of the discharge over time is called a **hydrograph**. The discharge is related to precipitation (Figure 39). When precipitation begins, the discharge usually increases rapidly to a peak and then decreases more slowly. Both surface runoff and throughflow contribute to the river discharge, but these die away fairly soon after the rain stops falling, eventually leaving only the base flow.

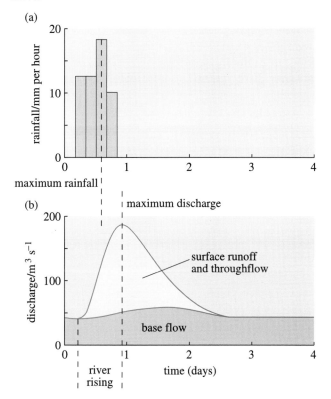

Figure 39 (a) A histogram of the rainfall during a storm, on a $100\,km^2$ catchment. (b) The hydrograph of river flow after the rainstorm in (a). There is a time difference between the time of maximum rainfall and the time of maximum discharge. The slope of a hydrograph is usually steeper when a river is rising than when it is falling.

51

The shape of a hydrograph depends on several factors:

1   *The size and shape of the catchment area.* The larger the catchment, the higher the peak discharge for a given rainfall and the longer the time difference between rainfall maximum and river discharge maximum. The steepness of the slope of the ground is also significant, as gentle slopes produce a longer time difference because the water runs off more slowly.

2   *The geology of the catchment*, particularly the permeability of the rocks. An impermeable catchment will produce higher peak discharges and lower flows at other times. In a permeable catchment, with a greater base-flow contribution, there is less variation in discharge.

3   *Climatic factors*, such as seasonal rainfall and melting snow. Figure 40 shows the types of hydrograph to be expected from different climatic regimes. (These hydrographs cover a year, whereas the hydrograph in Figure 39 is for a few days only.)

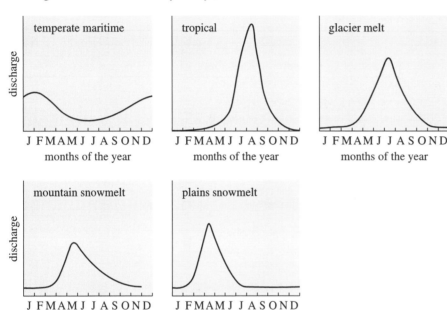

Figure 40   Theoretical yearly hydrographs for different climatic regimes in the northern hemisphere. The months of the year are indicated by their initial letters. The first two hydrographs are rainfall dependent; the others are temperature dependent.

The first two hydrographs in Figure 40 (temperate maritime and tropical) are dependent on *rainfall*. In temperate maritime climates (such as in the UK) rainfall occurs all the year, but evaporation is greater in summer, so there is a slightly greater discharge in winter than in summer. Within the tropics and in the equatorial zone there are usually wet and dry seasons, or even two wet seasons (Table 4, Section 2.2), and hydrographs are controlled by the rainfall pattern.

The other hydrographs in Figure 40 (glacier melt, mountain snowmelt and plains snowmelt) are dependent on *temperature*. When the catchment includes glaciers, the river flow is influenced by the melting conditions of the ice. Melting takes place mainly in the summer, giving peak discharges in June or July in the northern hemisphere. Melting of mountain snow starts earlier in the year, giving a peak discharge in May or June in the northern hemisphere. Snowmelt from plains (the interior regions of large continents) depends on latitude, with the more southerly rivers in the northern hemisphere having peak discharges in April in the northern hemisphere, and more northerly rivers having a peak in June. River hydrographs are often a combination of one or more of the climatic regimes in Figure 40.

4   *Vegetation and land use.* Our use of the land affects hydrographs, as described in the Box 'Land use and river discharge'.

Land use and river discharge

Changes to the land surface have varying effects on the surface runoff and infiltration characteristics of a catchment, and so can change the river discharge pattern.

Plants, especially trees, intercept precipitation and prevent it reaching the ground. An area that is forested also usually has a thick layer of decaying vegetation on the ground, which absorbs water, so plants, and forests in particular, reduce overland flow to rivers. Figure 41 compares the hydrographs for agricultural and forested catchments: the peak discharge is less in a forested area. Many upland reservoir catchments are forested, but as Figure 41 demonstrates, this may not be the best use for them, as afforestation reduces the total volume of water reaching a river, although making the flow more uniform.

Draining of wetlands or marshes removes water from the area more quickly, increasing the peak flow and runoff volume. The rapid removal of water reduces the time available for infiltration and may lower the water table, modifying the vegetation and changing the characteristics of the area.

Urbanization of land usually results in less infiltration and faster overland flow from buildings and roads, giving very high peak discharges on hydrographs (as Figure 41 shows) and sometimes the risk of flooding. To reduce this risk, and maintain the water table, newly urbanized areas (such as Milton Keynes) build lakes called balancing lakes, which increase infiltration.

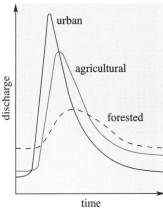

Figure 41 Theoretical hydrographs, each representing the same rainfall, for different land uses.

Question 18

Figure 42 is a hydrograph, covering a period of a year.

(a) Which climatic regime or regimes would produce a hydrograph of this shape?

(b) What is the maximum discharge and how many times greater than the average is it?

(c) What might be the cause of the high discharge peaks?

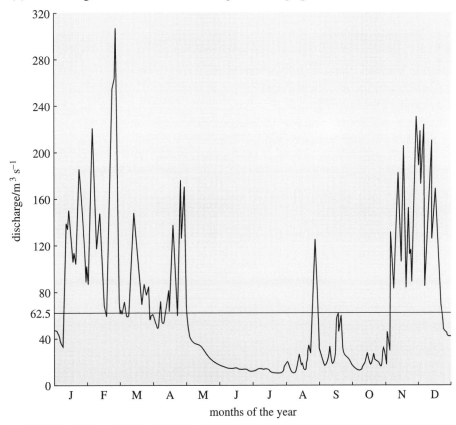

Figure 42
A hydrograph of a river, for use with Question 18. The horizontal line marks the average discharge for this river over a long period, and is $62.5\,\mathrm{m^3\,s^{-1}}$.

The river with the flow in Figure 42 discharges more water in the winter, whereas demand for water is higher in the hotter summer. To satisfy the summer demand, water must be stored during the winter and spring.

4.3 Reservoirs

The simplest and oldest way of storing surface water is in reservoirs and this has been done for thousands of years. Most reservoirs are still built to increase water supplies, but some are also built for other purposes, especially for generating hydroelectric power and for protection against floods. The Tennessee River in the United States, for example, has reservoirs to trap and store water that would otherwise cause floods, the water being released when the height of the river falls to safe levels. The Aswan High Dam in Egypt is used both to generate electricity and reduce flooding, as well as to provide water for irrigation.

4.3.1 River regulation

The older reservoirs in Britain are **direct supply reservoirs**; they store water for steady release by pipeline to the public supply. Many of the newer reservoirs are for **river regulation**; stored water is released into rivers when the natural discharge is low, so that it can be abstracted for use further downstream. The river itself transports the water from the reservoir so a pipeline is unnecessary. The discharge in winter exceeds requirements, but by storing, the scheme provides more water in summer than is naturally available in the river. The Clywedog reservoir on a tributary of the River Severn, for example, was built to store up to 50 million cubic metres of water in winter, releasing it during the summer. This is needed because, as Figure 42 shows, the summer discharge is only around $20\,\mathrm{m^3\,s^{-1}}$ at Bewdley, whereas in winter about $100\,\mathrm{m^3\,s^{-1}}$ are discharged. Both direct supply reservoirs and river regulation reservoirs may be **pumped storage reservoirs**, which do not fill naturally from a river, but have water pumped up to them. Many of the reservoirs in the Thames Valley are pumped storage reservoirs.

4.3.2 Sites for reservoirs

The simplest way to create a reservoir is to build a dam across a river where it flows through a narrow, deep valley. This shape of valley would enable a considerable volume of water to be stored, without flooding a large area of land or building a long dam. However, it is not always possible to find such a suitable site: a narrow, deep valley may not exist, or it may be too far from where the water is needed. A wide valley needing a long dam may have to be used, or even a flat lowland area that would need a low earth embankment surrounding most, if not all, of a shallow reservoir occupying a large area of land.

In practice, the following factors have to be considered when choosing a site for a water supply reservoir:
1 an adequate supply of high-quality water;
2 minimum detrimental effects on the environment;
3 elevation to provide a natural flow of water to the distribution system;
4 a reasonably watertight reservoir base and sides;
5 no geological hazards due to instability of the sides of the valley or earthquakes;
6 a suitable site for a dam.

The most important of these requirements are an adequate supply of water (1), preferably though not necessarily of high quality, and minimal

The Colorado River

The change in river discharge caused by river regulation reservoirs can be seen on a hydrograph of the Colorado River in the USA (Figure 43). The Colorado is a large river (its discharge is about ten times greater than the River Severn, shown in Figure 42) and has great seasonal fluctuations: in some years, such as 1920, its discharge varies from 50 to 2600 $m^3 s^{-1}$. This seasonal variation is caused by mountain snowmelt in the upper parts of the Colorado catchment in Wyoming, Colorado and Utah.

Downstream, at the hydrograph site on the Nevada–Arizona border, the Colorado River flows through desert and its water is very important, but most of this flow used to occur in the winter, when it was less useful for irrigated agriculture. Annual flooding was also common. To regulate the river flow, prevent flooding and to generate hydroelectric power, dams have been built on the Colorado to create reservoirs. The first major dam, the Hoover Dam (Plate 33), was completed in 1935, forming the reservoir of Lake Mead. This holds most of the spring snowmelt and prevents very high discharges and flooding.

● What was the highest discharge after the creation of Lake Mead reservoir?

○ It was about 800 $m^3 s^{-1}$, much lower than previous highs of up to 2800 $m^3 s^{-1}$ before 1935.

● How has Lake Mead affected the lower discharges of the Colorado?

○ These have increased, from general annual low values of 100–200 $m^3 s^{-1}$ before 1935 to 300–500 $m^3 s^{-1}$ from 1942 to 1955.

This is because of the use of Lake Mead as a river regulation reservoir: water is released downstream into the river at a more constant rate than in the unregulated flow. Lake Mead, as well as being used for river regulation, is also a direct supply reservoir, supplying water by pipeline to eastern Nevada, and for hydroelectric power generation.

Even after the completion of Lake Mead there were still times when floodwaters filled the Lake and were released downstream.

● Which were the years after 1935 when this happened?

○ There were peak discharges (although much lower than the pre-1935 peaks) in 1938, 1942, 1953 and 1958.

Another major reservoir was created further upstream of Lake Mead to trap this excess floodwater in 1963 (Lake Powell; Figure 43). Like Lake Mead, Lake Powell is used for direct supply and hydroelectric power as well as river regulation. Since 1963, although there are still seasonal variations in flow, these are relatively small, with maximum flows of around 400 $m^3 s^{-1}$ and minimum flows of around 200 $m^3 s^{-1}$.

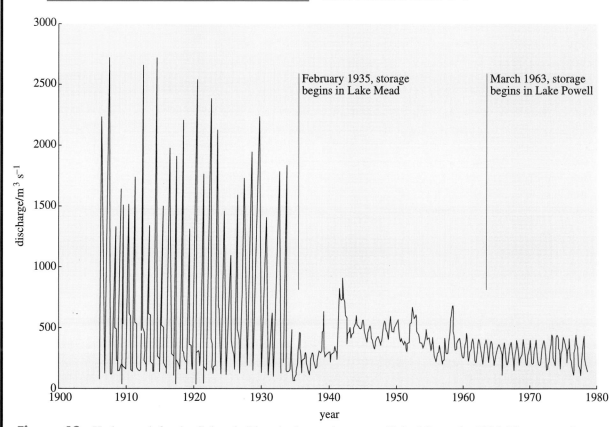

Figure 43 Hydrograph for the Colorado River in the south-western United States for 1906–79, measured downstream of the Hoover Dam. The reservoir behind the Hoover Dam is Lake Mead.

environmental implications (2). All the other requirements can be met, although it may be expensive to do so: water can be treated to improve its quality (1), or pumped to a higher level (3), and geological problems such as leakage (4) and instability (5) can be minimized.

The possibility of detrimental ecological or environmental effects can provoke much opposition to plans for new reservoirs, but if the need for a reservoir is great enough and there are no alternative areas, the reservoir is usually built. For example, the proposal to build the Aswan High Dam provoked opposition not only in Egypt but also world-wide, partly on the ground that it would drown the ancient temples of Abu Simbel. The dam was nevertheless constructed, and some of the temples were moved.

The requirements that the area be watertight, have minimal geological hazards, and be a suitable site for a dam, all involve considering the area's geology. Watertightness is affected by the permeability of the underlying rocks as well as by the geological structure of the area, the nature of any superficial deposits and the position of the water table.

If the underlying rocks are permeable, water may be lost from the reservoir by infiltration. Rocks with low permeability, suitable for reservoir areas, include clay-rich rocks, and most igneous and metamorphic rocks, provided they are not too highly fractured. However, reservoirs are sometimes built in areas with less suitable rocks, such as sandstone or limestone, if no more suitable rocks are available. Such areas can be made more watertight by lining the floor with clay or injecting concrete into permeable zones, although this is very expensive.

Problems of geological structure are not so easy to deal with. It is not usually possible to seal faults completely in the rocks under the area and some water may escape through them. If the rocks dip or are folded, water may be lost from the reservoir through the valley sides or floor, or beneath the dam.

Figure 44a shows an empty reservoir. As the reservoir fills, the water table in any surrounding permeable rocks will rise, as the level of a water table is closely related to that of any surface water, such as the reservoir. If the new water table beneath the surrounding hills slopes away from the reservoir (Figure 44b), groundwater will flow away from the reservoir until the water table has stabilized at a yet higher level (Figure 44c).

Most valley floors are covered with superficial deposits such as gravel, clay or peat. These usually have to be removed from the dam site so that the dam can be given a strong foundation in the underlying rock. Peat should be removed from the whole reservoir area as it is acidic and would affect the colour and quality of the water; but clays may be useful, as they are impermeable and can seal underlying permeable rocks.

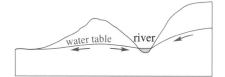

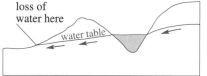

Figure 44 (a) Before the reservoir has filled. Groundwater flows towards the valley from both sides (blue arrows).

(b) Just after the reservoir has filled. The water table on either side of the valley has risen with the water level in the reservoir, so that the water table on the left now slopes down away from the reservoir. There will therefore be a loss of water from the reservoir by groundwater flow.

(c) The final situation. The water table has risen under the hill (due to infiltration) to a higher level than the reservoir surface. The water table slopes down into the reservoir, so groundwater flows towards the reservoir and water is no longer lost from the reservoir by groundwater flow.

Reservoirs may contribute to the danger of landslides where a reservoir is sited on bedrock strata that dip towards the reservoir. The rocks on the right of the reservoir in Figure 45 are inclined towards it and consist of alternating sand and shale bands. The sandstones are permeable, and water in them percolates down to the shale bands. The shale bands are impermeable, so the water builds up above the shale until eventually it may act as a lubricant, allowing the sandstone above to slide off down the hill into the reservoir.

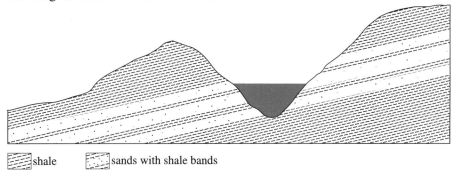

shale   sands with shale bands

Figure 45 Bands of shale provide planes on which rocks can slide. Therefore if rocks dip towards the reservoir, as on the right-hand side of the figure, there may be a danger of landslides into the reservoir. This danger is increased by the presence of the reservoir which raises the water level in the rocks on either side of the valley (see Figure 44).

Mines in the reservoir area present another possible hazard. Mines which are still being worked may be flooded by leakage from the reservoir, with much loss of life, or water may be lost from the reservoir by escaping into abandoned mines. The weight of the water or of the dam may also cause underlying mine workings to collapse, which in turn would damage the structure of the dam.

Question 19

Figure 46 shows five valleys, each with a different geological structure. Which valley(s), if any, might be suitable site(s) for a reservoir, and why?

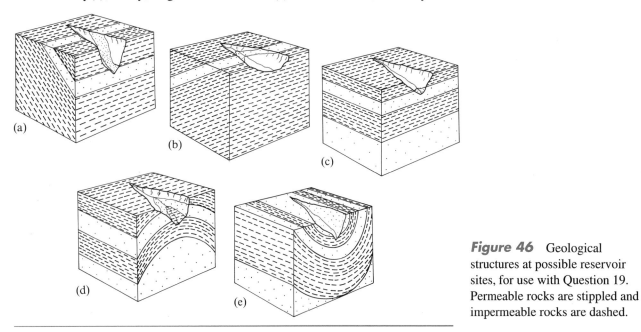

(a) (b) (c) (d) (e)

Figure 46 Geological structures at possible reservoir sites, for use with Question 19. Permeable rocks are stippled and impermeable rocks are dashed.

The Vaiont reservoir landslip

The Vaiont reservoir in Italy is in an area of limestones with marl bands (marl is a calcareous mudstone). After the reservoir had filled, the water table rose in the surrounding rocks, increasing the water pressure in the pores in the rock. This lubricated the beds of rock, and in 1963 caused a large landslide which dumped enormous amounts of rock into the reservoir from the flanking hillside (Plate 31). This displaced a huge volume of water which surged over the dam and also back up the valley, causing around six thousand deaths in nearby villages even though the dam itself remained intact.

4.3.3 Dams

To economize on constructional materials and costs, it is desirable to build a dam at a narrow part of a valley so that the dam can be kept as short as possible. The quantity of constructional materials needed to build dams, and their cost, can be enormous. The Aswan High Dam, built during the 1960s, cost £400 million for a 1.2 km dam. Though shorter than the Aswan High Dam, the longest dam in Britain, the Kielder Dam in Northumberland (Plate 32), which was completed in 1980, was part of a scheme costing £150 million.

There are two fundamental types of dam, which have different ways of withstanding the pressure of water in the reservoir behind them: **gravity dams** and **wall dams**. The gravity dam depends on its own weight to prevent deformation or movement, whereas the wall dam is a rigid structure that resists deformation and transfers the pressure of the water to the floor and sides of the valley. Some dams combine both types of feature.

The simplest form of gravity dam is made up of carefully selected unconsolidated material such as clay or broken rock. This is called an *earth* dam (although it is not made of garden-type earth!) Earth dams usually have an impermeable clay core to reduce the seepage of water through the dam, and the sides are usually covered with broken blocks of rock or concrete to reduce erosion by waves. Gravity dams can also be constructed entirely of piled-up masonry (stone blocks) or concrete. *Masonry* or *concrete* gravity dams are usually built if the reservoir site is a narrow valley, but if a reservoir has to be built in a wide valley or in a lowland area, earth dams are used as they are less expensive. Figure 47 shows how the Aswan High Dam, an earth dam, was built. The largest dam in Britain, the Kielder Dam, is also an earth dam (Plate 32).

Wall dams are usually built only in narrow valleys, when a relatively high dam is needed. They must be strong and impermeable, and are made of masonry or concrete. Their strength is often increased by making them curved in plan (convex towards the reservoir, just as curved arches are used to support heavy roofs in churches), or with buttresses on the downriver side (similar to those used to stop church walls falling outwards), or by reinforcing them internally with steel cables. The Hoover Dam on the Colorado River is an example of a wall dam (Plate 33).

Seepage below dams can be reduced by a **cutoff curtain** or an **apron**. A cutoff curtain is a narrow impermeable layer, usually made of concrete, extending below the dam, which reduces horizontal seepage of water under the dam (Figures 47 and 48a). The cutoff curtain extends downwards to a distance that is usually greater than the height of the dam, and if possible it goes down into impermeable rock. An apron is a horizontal impermeable layer at the foot of the dam wall which reduces downward seepage from the reservoir (Figure 48b).

Figure 47 Aswan High Dam on the River Nile, Egypt, shown in cross-section. This rockfilled gravity dam is 1.2 km long. It incorporates an upstream cofferdam (A) and a downstream cofferdam (B). The cutoff curtain extends to a depth equal to one-and-a-half times the height of the central dam ridge. The water levels shown are the highest expected. (Cofferdams and cutoff curtains are explained in the text.)

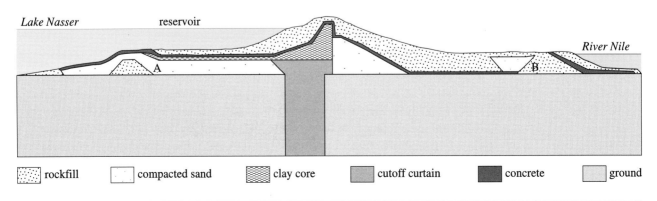

(a) 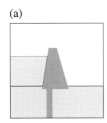 (b)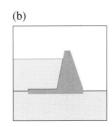

Figure 48 Two methods of reducing seepage under dams. (a) A cutoff curtain — an impervious layer slotted into the foundation. (b) An apron — an impervious layer laid horizontally in front of the upstream face.

One of the problems of building a dam in the valley of a major river lies in excluding water from the dam site while the dam is being built. Small temporary dams, called **cofferdams**, are often constructed for this purpose, and are sometimes incorporated into the main dam (Figures 47 and 49).

Figure 49 The Kariba Dam under construction in 1957 on the River Zambezi. The water is excluded by the circular cofferdam from the part of the dam under construction. This cofferdam was included in the final dam structure. There used to be another cofferdam in the part of the dam that includes the sluice gates, on the right-hand side of the river; but this was dismantled before the cofferdam shown in the picture was built.

4.3.4 *Environmental effects of reservoir construction*

Large reservoirs can totally alter the water resources of a country. Before the Aswan Dam was completed in Egypt, more than half of the 8×10^{10} cubic metres of water that flowed down the River Nile through Egypt each year ran into the sea. Now, about 80% of the water is used in Egypt, mainly for irrigation, and instead of a single annual crop grown after seasonal flooding, more than one crop can be grown each year. However, advantages such as these must be considered in conjunction with the environmental side-effects of reservoir construction. The major side-effects are:

1 *Land use* By their very nature, reservoirs occupy large areas of land. Lake Nasser, the reservoir created by the Aswan Dam, has an area of $6000\,km^2$, and even in Britain some $250\,km^2$ of land is covered by reservoirs. The largest reservoir in Britain — indeed in western Europe — is Kielder Water in Northumberland, which covers about $10.5\,km^2$. British reservoirs are generally in upland areas of scenic beauty that are otherwise suitable only for hiking and related pastimes, and as rough grazing for sheep, but reservoirs may cover up rich farmland or villages, or destroy a site of outstanding natural beauty or of archaeological importance. Land itself is an important resource, and drowning it under a reservoir may be not the best use of that resource, especially if the water can be supplied by alternative means.

2 *Ecological changes* Creation of a reservoir produces ecological changes not only to the area of the reservoir itself, by destroying the

59

natural vegetation, but also upstream and downstream of the reservoir. The gradient of a river upstream of a reservoir may be reduced, so the water will slow down. This changes the character of the river, may cause deposition of sediment, and changes to the natural vegetation and animal life. Downstream of the reservoir the discharge will change, as well as the sediment load, also affecting the plants and animals. For example, annual flooding may cease.

3   *Dam failure*   Dams may collapse, releasing large amounts of water downstream, causing destruction of buildings and killing people and animals. Collapse may be caused by inappropriate construction, failure of the underlying sediments or rock, overfilling or earthquakes. Earthquake damage to dams is rare but does occur. Although China, for example, has thousands of dams in earthquake areas, none has collapsed in recent years from earthquake damage, but in Britain, an area of low earthquake activity, the Earl's Burn Dam near Stirling failed following an earthquake in 1839.

4   *Sediment filling*   The lifetime of reservoirs can vary greatly. Many reservoirs have lasted for over a hundred years, but some may be useful for only a much shorter period — fifty years or so — not because of the general deterioration of the dam as it gets older, but because the sediment accumulates in the reservoir. Rivers carry large amounts of mud, silt and sand in suspension, particularly during floods, and when a river enters a reservoir it slows down, so that the sediment it has been carrying in suspension is deposited on the floor of the reservoir. Lake Mead, on the Colorado River, has had its storage capacity reduced by over a half since the dam was completed in 1935. This is less of a problem for British reservoirs, as rivers here are smaller and carry much less sediment. The Derwent Valley reservoirs (see Section 6.1.3) have had their volumes reduced by less than 1% through sedimentation in the 60 years since they were completed. Some water-supply reservoirs are constructed so that sediment-laden floodwaters can bypass the reservoir, but obviously this is not possible where the reservoirs are intended for flood control.

5   *Sediment loss to agriculture*   The trapping of sediment behind dams may also affect agriculture. The Nile Valley, for example, used to flood naturally once a year, and the sediment in the waters was deposited on the

---

The St Francis Dam failure

The St Francis Dam was a wall dam, completed in 1926, and built in a valley about 70 km north of Los Angeles in California. The dam was 60 m high and 150 m in width. The reservoir behind the dam was intended for water supply. The rocks to one side of the valley were sandstones and other sedimentary rocks, and to the other side were schists (metamorphic rocks that tend to break along parallel planes) which sloped down towards the dam and reservoir. The contact between the two rock types was a fault, along the line of the valley floor, and the dam was built over this.

The dam abruptly failed on 12 March 1928, and the water released drowned several hundred people and caused $10 million of damage.

The failure was caused by change in strength of the rocks as they became saturated with water. The rocks were strong when dry, but the water table rose in the surrounding rocks as the reservoir filled (as in Figure 44c), and the water dissolved out the cement holding the sedimentary rocks together. Eventually the rock collapsed, taking one side of the dam with it. As water began to pour out of the reservoir, it eroded the base of the schists, which slid into the valley, and the other side of the dam collapsed. Surprisingly, the central section of the dam remained standing!

You may be astonished (as I am) that a dam was ever built in this valley as it seems to have so many inappropriate features — porous sedimentary rocks, metamorphic rocks that could slide into the valley, and a fault.

land, forming a fertile soil. These floodwaters and the sediment they carry are now trapped behind the Aswan Dam, and artificial fertilizers must be used downriver in the valley.

Without the yearly supply of sediment in floodwater, the banks of the Nile are eroding downstream of the dam, and the Nile delta is reducing in size, the erosion by wave action no longer being counteracted by a fresh supply of sediment.

6 *Soil salinization* The change from annual flooding by a river to perennial irrigation can also cause soil salinization, if salts normally present in the river water accumulate in the soil as the water evaporates. These salts were previously washed away by the flooding, but the reduced supply of water by irrigation leaves them in the soil. The water is taken in by the plants, or evaporated by the Sun, leaving the salts behind. This causes a decline in crop yields until eventually the soil becomes useless for agriculture. It is prevented by using enough irrigation water to wash the salts through the soil, and draining this water from the fields.

7 *Induced earthquakes* Some reservoirs *cause* earthquakes to occur. This is perhaps not so surprising, as earthquakes are caused by stress in rocks, and the addition of a large mass of water in a reservoir on top of the rocks at the Earth's surface stresses the rocks and can trigger an earthquake. Not all reservoirs induce earthquakes: it is in general only the larger reservoirs, or the deepest ones (over 100 m deep) and only if the reservoir is built in an earthquake area, releasing stress already stored in the region.

Induced earthquakes mainly occur during *changes* in water level in a reservoir, during initial filling (this occurred for Lake Nasser) or during seasonal changes of water level.

Reservoirs that have induced earthquakes include Marathon, Greece (1938), Lake Mead, USA (1939), Kariba, Rhodesia (now Zimbabwe) (1963), Lake Nasser, Egypt (1965, 1981), and Kremasta, Greece (1966).

The Narmada River scheme: salvation or an environmental disaster?

The Narmada River flows through the drought-prone states of Gujarat and Madhya Pradesh in western India. A project is under way to build 30 major dams on the river, along with smaller ones over the next 50 years, to generate drinking water for the region, to irrigate 18 000 km^2 of land, to protect the area from flooding and to generate 1450 megawatts of hydroelectric power. Its estimated cost is around \$40 000 million and will be partly funded by the World Bank. It is an enormous scheme and has attracted strong support but also violent opposition.

The dams, when completed, will submerge 2000 km^2 of fertile land and 1500 km^2 of forest, and will displace around 200 000 people.

The scheme is enormously popular with the political parties in the local Indian States, which will benefit from the extra water and electricity. It is also popular with those many people who have had to walk miles to collect water each day and who do not have enough water to irrigate their crops. It is obviously not popular with those forced to move from villages that will be submerged, or environmental organizations. One of the more prominent 'green' Indian politicians has called the scheme an 'environmental catastrophe'.

The opponents' case is that the same benefits could be gained by a less grandiose scheme of local irrigation projects, which could do the same job at a fraction of the cost, and with minimal environmental damage. There is also the question of **sustainable development**: a sustainable resource is one that can be supplied not only indefinitely, but also without causing irreversible damage to the environment. More rigorously, sustainable development is defined as 'Development that meets the needs of the present without compromising the ability of future generations to meet their own needs.' Environmentalist opponents to the Narmada scheme argue that it is non-sustainable, given the environmental side-effects and the fear that the necessary maintenance of the dams, reservoirs and irrigation canals may not be carried out.

4.4 Summary of Section 4

1 Many rivers originate from springs, which occur at points where groundwater reaches the surface. Springs can occur in different geological settings, forming artesian springs, valley springs, stratum springs or solution channel springs.

2 The water in a river originates from overland flow (resulting from precipitation and springs), from throughflow (which is water that has moved through the soil, above the water table), and from base flow (which is groundwater discharged directly into the river). The base flow forms a higher proportion of river water in summer than in winter, and in rivers flowing over good aquifers. The discharge of a river at any point is usually determined by first measuring the stage, which is the water level in the river, and then reading off a value for the discharge from the rating curve, which is a plot of measured discharge for various stages. A river hydrograph is a record of the discharge over a period of time. The shape of a short-period hydrograph (the record for a few days) depends on the size, shape, geology, vegetation and land use of the river catchment. The shape of the long-period hydrograph (e.g. for a year) depends primarily on the type of climate in the region of the river.

3 Reservoirs increase the amount of water stored on the land surface. Water-supply reservoirs can be used as direct supply reservoirs or for river regulation. Reservoirs may also be built solely or partly for other purposes, such as the generation of hydroelectricity or for flood prevention. The criteria for selecting sites for water-supply reservoirs are a good supply of high-quality water, minimum ecological and environmental disturbance, a high elevation, a watertight reservoir area, no geological hazards and a suitable dam site. The most suitable reservoir sites are narrow, deep valleys, but reservoirs often have to be built in wider valleys or in flat lowland areas.

4 There are two types of dams, gravity dams and wall dams. The gravity dam depends on its own weight to prevent deformation, whereas the wall dam is a rigid structure that transfers the pressure of the water to the floor and sides of a valley.

5 The environmental effects of constructing a reservoir include the loss of a large area of land, ecological changes, dam failure, sediment filling, sediment loss to agriculture, soil salinization and induced earthquakes.

Question 20

Hydrographs for many of the rivers in Britain are similar to the top left hydrograph in Figure 40, the temperate maritime regime. Is the shape of this hydrograph due to a seasonal variation in precipitation, or due to a different cause?

Question 21

Estimate the percentage contributed by the base flow to the discharge of the River Severn at Bewdley (Figure 42), for (a) the months November–April and (b) the months May–October. Give your answers to the nearest 10%. You may need to refer to Figure 39b to identify the base-flow component of the hydrograph.

Activity 6

(a) Sketch three north-west to south-east cross-sections of the aquifer passing through points A, B and C of Figure 36. Each section should show the ground surface, the base of the aquifer, the water table, the river and the groundwater flow directions.

(b) On the basis of your answer to (a), between which points, approximately, would you expect to find water in the river channel, at the time of year depicted in Figure 36? Explain your answer.

5 WATER QUALITY

To judge what actually constitutes poor quality or polluted water, we must first understand what the properties of naturally occurring waters are. Natural water is not just H_2O: all natural waters contain dissolved and suspended substances. Water **pollution** is defined as a change in the quality of the water due to human activity that makes the water less suitable for use than it was originally. It is difficult to set absolute standards of purity, however, because water that is considered clean enough for one purpose may be too polluted for another.

5.1 Natural waters

Rainwater, seawater and river water (Figure 50) and groundwaters (Figure 51) generally have very different chemical compositions. They may also differ widely in their concentrations of **total dissolved solids (TDS)**. Average TDS values are: $7\,mg\,l^{-1}$ for rainwater, $118\,mg\,l^{-1}$ for river water, various values for groundwater, and $34\,400\,mg\,l^{-1}$ for seawater. The concentration of total dissolved solids is a good indicator of water

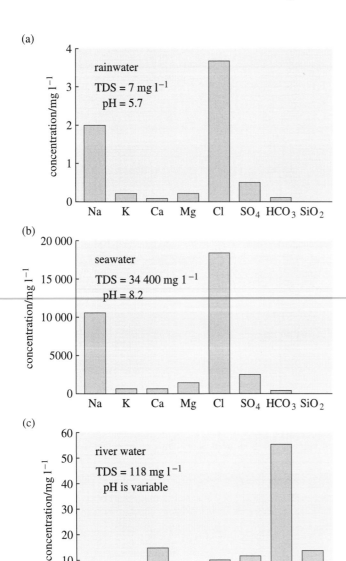

Figure 50 The average chemical compositions of rainwater, seawater and river water. Only the major dissolved constituents are shown, and dissolved gases are not included. Different scales are used for each histogram. River water may vary considerably from the composition shown here.

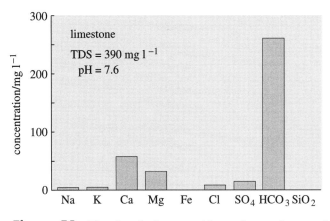
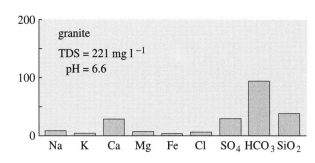

Figure 51 The chemical compositions of groundwaters from a limestone and a granite.

---

pH

pH is a measure of how acidic or alkaline a solution is. The pH scale ranges from 1 to 14, with low values the most acid, and high values the most alkaline. A neutral solution (or pure water) has a pH value of 7.

An acidic solution has a higher concentration of hydrogen ions, H⁺, than pure water (this is where the 'H' in the term 'pH' comes from). For example,

when carbon dioxide (CO_2) dissolves in water, a slightly acidic solution is formed:

$$H_2O + CO_2 = H^+ + HCO_3^-$$
$$\text{bicarbonate}$$

The pH of most natural waters lies between 5.5 and 8.5.

---

quality, and standards that have been set for drinking water and for water used in other ways include maximum values for TDS (Section 5.4).

Rainwater and seawater (Figure 50a and b) have similar relative proportions of dissolved solids, although rainwater is much more dilute. This is because most of the dissolved salts in rainwater come from sea spray into the atmosphere. A major difference in composition is the greater relative proportions of dissolved gases in rainwater, particularly carbon dioxide. Natural rainwater is slightly acidic as a result of this reaction, with an average pH of 5.65, whereas the average pH of seawater is 8.2 (see Box on 'pH'). Rainwater may be even more acidic in areas where the highly soluble acidic gases sulphur dioxide and nitrogen dioxide (which are produced by fossil fuel power generation, transport and industrial processes) are present in the atmosphere; this will be considered in more detail in Block 4 *Energy 1*.

River water and groundwater differ from rainwater in that both have greater TDS values and different relative proportions of dissolved substances (Figures 50c and 51). Rivers may also contain solid particles in suspension, in addition to dissolved substances. Groundwater usually has a low content of suspended solids because these have been filtered out as the water passes through the ground. Organic processes in soils, the solution of soluble minerals in rocks, interaction with clays and other minerals, and the chemical weathering of rocks are responsible for the changes in composition as rainwater becomes surface water or groundwater. The relative proportions of the dissolved substances change and the TDS value increases as a result of these processes. In general, groundwater takes on the properties of rocks through which it passes.

 What are the three principal dissolved constituents of river water and groundwater from Figures 50c and 51?

For the river water and granitic groundwater the three most abundant are bicarbonate (HCO_3^-), calcium (Ca^{2+}) and silica (SiO_2). For the limestone groundwater, magnesium (Mg^{2+}) is more abundant than silica.

The main reason for the abundance of HCO_3^- and Ca^{2+} is the solution of calcium carbonate present as limestone or as cement in sandstone. Limestone ($CaCO_3$) is a fairly common rock, and it dissolves readily in acidic waters such as rainwater:

$$CaCO_3 + H^+ = Ca^{2+} + HCO_3^-$$

The mineral dolomite ($CaMg(CO_3)_2$) has a similar reaction in acidic water, and provides a source of magnesium ions. Magnesium also comes from the weathering of minerals such as pyroxene. Silica comes from the weathering of silicates, which are a major constituent of most common rocks.

Hardness in water

Hardness in water is mainly due to the presence of ions of the elements calcium, magnesium and iron. High concentrations of these ions have objectionable side-effects, particularly scum and scaling. The ions react with soap, forming insoluble compounds and preventing the soap from lathering properly, causing rings on bathtubs and leaving a grey soap scum on washed clothes. Hard water also leaves mineral deposits (scale) in plumbing and water-using appliances, particularly kettles.

If the principal dissolved anion in hard in water is bicarbonate, carbonate salts of the metals are precipitated when the water is boiled or heated above 70 °C. Such water is said to possess temporary hardness because the carbonate salts are largely insoluble and are thus removed from the water, and deposited as a scale.

$$Ca^{2+} + 2HCO_3^- \xrightarrow{\text{heat}} H_2O + CO_2 + CaCO_3$$

calcium carbonate (scale)

When the main anions present are chloride, sulphate or nitrate, the hardness is called permanent hardness, which cannot be removed by boiling. Although this type of hardness also contributes to scaling, in this case the precipitate that is formed is due to the decreased solubility of calcium sulphate at higher temperatures and not to the formation of new insoluble compounds.

Many people in hard water areas use water softeners, which usually replace calcium, magnesium, and certain other ions from water with sodium ions. The sodium ions are replenished from the salt (sodium chloride) supply in the water softener. While softened water containing sodium ions in moderate concentration is unobjectionable in taste or household use, it may be of concern to those on diets involving restricted sodium intake.

In spite of the problems encountered when boiling and using soap in hard water, the dissolved solids give such water a pleasant taste and have various medicinal benefits.

The extent of hard water in Britain tends to follow a north to south-east gradient; the softest water is in Scotland, northern England and Wales, and the hardest in East Anglia and south-east England. Mortality from cardiovascular (CV) disease (heart disease and stroke) tends to follow the same pattern — a higher rate in the north and north-west than the south and the south-east. Several statistical surveys have shown an inverse relationship between CV disease and water hardness. After adjustment for socio-economic and climatic factors this relationship is somewhat weakened but remains statistically significant. It can be shown that towns with *very* soft water ($CaCO_3$ concentration below $25\,mg\,l^{-1}$) have a CV mortality 10–15% higher than in areas with harder water (above $170\,mg\,l^{-1}\,CaCO_3$), while any further increase in hardness above these figures does not additionally lower CV mortality. This association of CV disease with soft water districts may be influenced by either water hardness itself or by some factor closely associated with it. The EU has set restrictive levels of water softening, and UK drinking water should now have a minimum hardness, *if* it has been softened, of $150\,mg\,l^{-1}$ of calcium carbonate.

Other reactions, involving different minerals, account for the remaining dissolved substances in surface water and groundwaters. The final composition of the water will depend on the precise reactions that have taken place, and will vary with the type of rock the water has flowed over or through. Water flowing through igneous and metamorphic rocks usually has lower TDS values than that through sedimentary rocks, because igneous and metamorphic rocks contain minerals that are generally less soluble. Water that has flowed through deposits of ore minerals will often have a high metal ion content and may have a high sulphate content, derived from sulphide ore minerals.

The TDS value of the water also depends on the length of time the water has been in contact with rock. The residence time of groundwater is generally higher than that of surface water (Table 3, Section 2.1), so groundwaters usually have higher TDS values. The composition of groundwater changes as it passes through an aquifer. Near the recharge area the groundwater has low TDS values, but as the water flows through the aquifer it gains more dissolved substances, so the TDS values are usually highest at discharge points. The chemistry of groundwater can therefore be used to trace the flow of water. For example, if the TDS is measured in a number of wells in an area, the TDS contours can be plotted in the same ways as for depths of the water table, and it can be assumed that groundwater will flow in the direction of greatest concentration. Contours can also be drawn for individual substances in the water.

In hot dry regions where the rainfall is low and evaporation is high (arid regions), there is little infiltration and the soluble salts and soluble products of chemical weathering are flushed from aquifers very slowly. So the groundwater can have high TDS values in these areas.

Deeper groundwaters that are slow moving often have particularly high concentrations of dissolved substances, with TDS values above a few thousand milligrams per litre. Sodium chloride is usually a major constituent of these waters. Either the waters form when meteoric water dissolves salt deposits, or possibly they may incorporate formation water, which was originally seawater that was trapped in sediments during their formation. When these saline waters are discharged at the surface they are often called **mineral waters**.

⬤ Looking back at Figure 51, why does the groundwater from the limestone area have a higher TDS value than the groundwater from the granite area ?

◯ Limestone is much more soluble (in acidic waters) than the minerals in granite. The high TDS is caused mainly by calcium and bicarbonate ions.

The variation in natural waters makes it hard to determine when water is polluted. Although pollution means a deterioration in water quality caused by human agencies, the same *effect* may occur naturally. For instance, during rainstorms large amounts of sediment and vegetable matter can be washed into rivers; toxic metals and acid waters can get into rivers and groundwaters where concentrations of ore minerals outcrop; and contamination can result where oil seeps out at the surface. These are all natural processes, and many of the effects will cure themselves in time; the environment has ways of adapting itself to such long-term effects. Pollution caused by humans, on the other hand, can be on a very large scale, can happen rapidly, can take a variety of forms, and upset the ecological balance where it occurs.

5.2 Pollutants

We shall now look at the most common water pollutants, their sources, their effects, and how they can be controlled. A summary is provided in Table 6 and some points are discussed below in more detail.

5.2.1 Natural organic material

The natural organic material found as a pollutant in water has come from domestic sewage and the effluent of farms and food-processing industries. Farm waste can be especially polluting and is an important EU issue: cattle slurry is up to 100 times as polluting per cubic metre as domestic sewage, and silage effluent is up to 200 times as polluting. Natural organic material consists of carbohydrates, proteins and fats, plus a number of other substances in lesser amounts. These are biodegradable; that is, they can be broken down by bacteria and other organisms into relatively harmless end-products. If sufficient oxygen is present in the water, aerobic bacteria (oxygen-using bacteria) feed on the organic material, using oxygen dissolved in the water. The polluting material is converted into water, carbon dioxide (CO_2), nitrates (NO_3^-), sulphates (SO_4^{2-}) and phosphates (PO_4^{3-}). This process can continue as long as the bacteria can get enough oxygen from the water.

The oxygen concentration of natural fresh water is around $10\,mg\,l^{-1}$. The concentration depends partly on the rate at which oxygen is supplied by aquatic plants through photosynthesis and partly on the rate at which it is dissolved from the air — more oxygen is dissolved where there is a proportionately large surface area of water in contact with the air, such as in shallow ponds or turbulent rivers. Another important influence on oxygen concentration is temperature. The higher the temperature, the lower the amount of dissolved oxygen in the water: at $10\,°C$ the concentration is about $11\,mg\,l^{-1}$, falling to about $9\,mg\,l^{-1}$ at $20\,°C$.

If excessive amounts of natural organic materials are discharged into a body of water, the demands of the bacteria feeding on it exceed the rate at which the oxygen can be replenished, and the oxygen concentration falls. This brings about a reduction in aquatic life; many animals in the water will die as the oxygen concentration decreases, and few plants thrive when organic pollution is severe. Trout and salmon die when the oxygen concentration falls below $3\,mg\,l^{-1}$, and aerobic bacteria will not survive at concentrations below about $0.5\,mg\,l^{-1}$.

At this point the decomposition of the polluting organic material is taken over by anaerobic bacteria (bacteria that exist in the absence of oxygen). These bacteria reduce the organic material to a different set of end-products — methane (CH_4), ammonia (NH_3) and hydrogen sulphide (H_2S). They give the water a foul smell and indicate severe pollution.

A measure of how much natural organic material — sewage, sewage effluent or industrial effluent — can be safely discharged into a river or lake is the **biochemical oxygen demand (BOD)**. This is defined as the amount of oxygen taken up by micro-organisms (principally bacteria) in decomposing the organic material in a sample stored in darkness for 5 days at $20\,°C$. The higher the BOD, the more the material will decrease the level of dissolved oxygen in the water into which it is discharged.

Rivers have some capacity for self-purification after pollution by biodegradable, natural organic materials. Figure 52 shows the effects of pollution from a sewage outfall on one particular river.

Table 6 The nature, sources, effects and control of some major types of pollutants

Pollutant	Nature	Common sources	Effects of pollution	Control
natural organic material	biodegradable organic materials; normally decomposed by aerobic bacteria (which require water-dissolved oxygen)	domestic sewage; food-processing industries; farms	excessive depletion of oxygen in water damages aquatic life; complete removal of oxygen causes anaerobic bacterial action on pollutants, resulting in offensive smells	sewage treatment works
living organisms	disease-causing organisms (bacteria, viruses)	human and animal wastes; certain industries (e.g. tanning, slaughtering)	purification treatment needed to obtain potable supplies; curtailed recreational uses of rivers, lakes, etc.	most commonly controlled with chlorine; seldom possible to remove all bacterial and viral contamination, but concentrations are greatly reduced
plant nutrients	principally nitrogen and phosphorous compounds	domestic sewage; industrial wastes; farms (especially from chemical fertilizers)	excessive growth of aquatic plant life leading to oxygen-demanding pollution, offensive smells, bad taste; excess nitrogen in drinking water could be toxic	serious problem: not removed by ordinary sewage treatment methods; very expensive to reduce
organic chemicals	detergents, herbicides, pesticides, industrial by-products	domestic sewage and industrial waste; farms	threat to fish and other wildlife; possible long-term hazards to human beings	very often not removed by usual sewage or water purification treatments
inorganic chemicals	salt, acids, metallic salts, cyanides, etc.	mining; industrial processes; natural deposits (e.g. salt)	interference with manufacturing processes; toxic effects on humans and wildlife; bad smells and tastes; corrosion of equipment	difficult: special treatment necessary
sediments	primarily soils and minerals; also some industrial by-products	land erosion by storms; flood waters; some industrial, quarrying and mining processes	obstruction or filling of rivers, lakes, reservoirs; increased cost of water purification; interference with manufacturing processes; equipment corrosion; reduced aquatic life	controlled by use of soil conservation and flood control methods; also by improvement of industrial technology; reduced by settling lakes
heat	heated water returned to rivers and lakes	electric power plants; steel mills; refineries and other industrial cooling units	reduction of oxygen in the water, resulting in slower or incomplete pollutant decomposition and harm to aquatic life	minimized by recirculation and reuse of industrial cooling waters

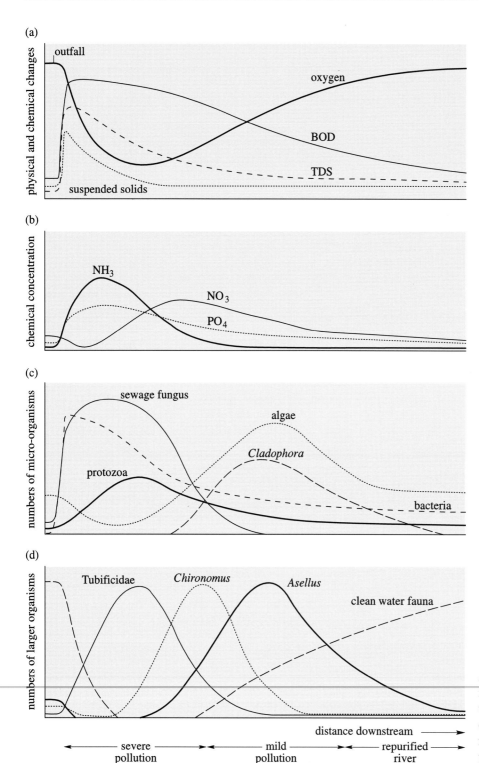

Figure 52 Typical changes in the chemistry and biology of the water in a river downstream of a sewage outfall. (You do not need to know details of the plants and animals in the river.)

Question 22

(a) Downstream from the sewage outfall, the dissolved oxygen in the water suddenly decreases and then gradually increases again (Figure 52a). How can this be explained?

(b) How and why do the concentrations of ammonia (NH_3) in Figure 52b vary?

(c) Which organisms appear to be most able to tolerate the pollution (Figures 52c and d)?

(d) What is the most likely explanation for the changes in the distribution of the organisms downstream of the sewage outfall?

5.2.2 *Living organisms*

Besides the living organisms that form part of the natural cycle in rivers, there are other organisms that are less desirable. Their presence is generally due to human activities, and they are a form of pollution. Most of these organisms are **pathogenic bacteria**, which can cause disease. The most common source of pathogenic bacteria is sewage, and the purpose of the earliest legislation prohibiting the discharge of raw sewage into rivers was to prevent the spread of disease. Pathogenic bacteria are adapted to body temperatures so they die off relatively quickly in cold river waters. For example, typhoid bacteria die within seven days in river water at the temperatures found in Britain — but a week is long enough to spread infection.

As well as bacteria, there are other aquatic organisms that may be harmful. Diseases may also be transmitted by protozoa, worms, snails and insect larvae.

Non-pathogenic bacteria form an essential part of the aquatic system. One such bacterium, *Escherichia coli,* lives in human and animal intestines, and therefore its presence in river water is a useful indication of faecal pollution. The **coliform count** (the number of coliform bacteria, of which *E. coli* is one, present in a fixed volume of water) is a measure of the extent of such pollution.

5.2.3 *Plant nutrients*

Plant nutrients are inorganic substances — mainly nitrogen and phosphorus compounds — that are essential for normal plant growth. Nitrogen and phosphorus come from human and animal faeces, detergents and fertilizers, and are not removed by normal water treatment processes or by sewage treatment. If the concentration of these nutrients exceeds the normal level in water they can cause a rapid proliferation of algae — an algal bloom. This can discolour the water, give it a bad taste and smell, and may produce a green scum on the surface. When they die, the algae sink and decay, forming large amounts of natural organic material with a high oxygen demand. The water becomes deoxygenated and polluted even further. This type of pollution is not usually a problem in British rivers but it does affect some reservoirs, lakes and canals.

5.2.4 *Organic and inorganic chemicals*

Organic and inorganic chemicals become pollutants when they are washed into rivers, lakes or the sea and affect organisms which they were not originally intended to come into contact with. Some of the chemicals are toxic (poisonous), depending on their concentrations. Toxic organic substances include agricultural pesticides, herbicides and bactericides such as DDT, dimethyl mercury and polychlorinated biphenyls (PCBs), which are by-products of the plastics industry. PCBs and DDT are particularly dangerous as they are very stable; they are not biodegradable so they can accumulate in water and in living organisms. Because of this, the use of DDT is now banned in most industrialized countries, although it is still used in most developing ones as it is a cheap and effective pesticide. Toxic inorganic substances include salts of the metals copper, silver, lead, gold, nickel, chromium, zinc, cadmium and mercury, and the metalloid arsenic. Many of these are toxic at low concentrations: less than $1\,\mathrm{mg\,l^{-1}}$. Most are wastes from industrial processes.

5.2.5 Heat

Heat has two main effects. As we mentioned when discussing natural organic pollutants, a rise in temperature brings about a decrease in the amount of oxygen dissolved in the water. At the same time the rise in temperature increases the metabolic rate of organisms and therefore their demand for oxygen.

Heat can also cause fish to spawn and hatch out of season and to alter their migration patterns. To avoid such problems, when heated water is returned to rivers after being used for cooling (in power stations, for example), there should always be a minimum flow in the river which is sufficient to dissipate the heat and keep the temperature rise to only a few degrees.

Before we move on to discuss the extent and effects of pollution, look again at Table 6. You now know the main pollutants and something about them. As you can see, a number of pollutants can arise from the same source.

Activity 7

List four main sources of pollution and for each source write a short paragraph about the types and effects of the pollution from that source.

5.3 The extent of water pollution

Water may become polluted by discharges (e.g. from sewage works or industry), overland flow (e.g. from farmland) or incidents (e.g. rupture of a farm slurry tank). Discharges in the UK require the consent of the pollution control authority: the National Rivers Authority in England and Wales, River Purification Boards in Scotland and the Environmental Protection Division of the Department of the Environment in Northern Ireland.

5.3.1 Surface water

The quality of surface water in the UK, represented by lengths of waterway in each quality class, is given in Table 7.

Table 7 Water quality in England and Wales in 1980, 1985 and 1990, in Scotland in 1980 and 1985, and in Northern Ireland in 1980, 1985 and 1989

England and Wales

Rivers and canals

Class	1980 (40 630 km) Length (%)	1985 (41 390 km) Length (%)	1990 (42 380 km) Length (%)
good 1A	34	33	29
good 1B	35	34	34
fair 2	21	24	25
poor 3	8	9	9
bad 4	2	2	2

Estuaries

Class	1980 (2730 km) Length (%)	1985 (2730 km) Length (%)	1990 (2720 km) Length (%)
good A	68	68	66
fair B	23	24	24
poor C	5	5	7
bad D	4	3	3

Scotland

Rivers and canals

Class	1980 (47 510 km) Length (%)	1985 (47 510 km) Length (%)
unpolluted	95	96
doubtful	4	4
poor	1	1
grossly polluted	–	–

Estuaries

Class	1980 (470 km) Length (%)	1985 (470 km) Length (%)
unpolluted	60	96
doubtful	28	4
poor	9	1
grossly polluted	6	–

Northern Ireland

Rivers

Class	1980 (1250 km) Length (%)	1985 (1390 km) Length (%)	1989 (1430 km) Length (%)
good 1A	23	15	25
good 1B	61	69	56
fair 2	13	11	14
poor 3	3	5	5
bad 4	–	–	–

Estuaries

Class	1985 (120 km) Length (%)
good A	83
fair B	–
poor C	17
bad D	–

The lengths given after each survey date are the total lengths of rivers, etc. surveyed: this may vary slightly in different surveys because of different classification criteria. Percentages may not add up to 100% due to rounding errors. In England and Wales, quality class 1A is for rivers of high quality, suitable for public water supply and game fisheries; 1B is rivers of less high quality than 1A but usable for substantially the same purposes; 2 is suitable for public water supply only after advanced treatment, and for coarse fisheries; 3 is poor quality, fish generally absent, may be used for low-grade industrial abstraction; 4 is highly polluted. Slightly different classifications apply in Scotland and Northern Ireland.

◐ How have the percentages of river lengths in the good quality classes 1A and 1B changed between 1980 and 1990 in England and Wales?

◑ In 1980, 69% was good quality, in 1990 it was 63% — an overall deterioration of water quality.

This deterioration is caused by a combination of greater discharges from sewage works, industry and farms, overland flow from farmland, and two years of low rainfall and hot summers. In the south-west, intensive agriculture is the main cause, producing large quantities of animal slurry and silage effluent. Drought and pollution from sewage works were the main causes in the Thames area.

In contrast, river quality surveys before 1980 showed a gradually improving quality: the Thames is an appropriate example of this (see Box 'The River Thames: pollution and cleanup').

Cleaning up polluted rivers or lakes is more complicated when they pass through more than one country. For example, the River Rhine flows through eight countries, and an almost total lack of pollution control has resulted in the Rhine being probably the most polluted large river in the world (see Box 'The River Rhine: international management of pollution').

The River Thames: pollution and cleanup

The River Thames at London has a high discharge (a dry weather flow of about $13\,\text{m}^3\,\text{s}^{-1}$), but receives vast amounts of sewage effluent. In the last century, untreated sewage was discharged into the Thames but as the population of London grew, the Thames became so polluted and unpleasant that the sewage had to be treated before being discharged into the river. Figure 53 shows the dissolved oxygen in the River Thames as a percentage of the maximum (saturated) value. A good quality river will have an oxygen level close to 100% saturation. But if a river is polluted, oxygen in the water will be used in the breakdown of organic pollutants (Section 5.2) and the oxygen concentration will fall. The oxygen in the river in Figure 52, for example, was reduced to about a quarter just downstream of the sewage outfall. Oxygen was almost absent over a 60 km stretch of the River Thames by the 1950s (Figure 53). This part of the river contained water of very poor quality, and fish were absent. Since the 1950s, however, more extensive and improved treatment of sewage before the effluent is discharged to the river has improved the quality of the water, and the whole river was class 1 or class 2 by 1981.

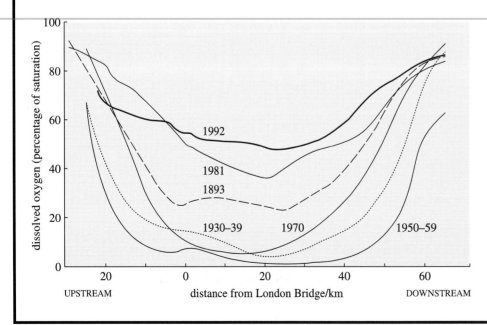

Figure 53 Dissolved oxygen in the River Thames between 1893 and 1992 for the months July to October, when discharge is low and pollution is greatest.

The River Rhine: international management of pollution

Until recently, countries have tended to dump waste into the River Rhine and then leave it to be dealt with by the next country downstream. There are 40 million inhabitants in the highly industrialized Rhine river basin, and their domestic and industrial wastes, often untreated, go into the river. The Rhine river basin covers 225 000 km^2 and includes eight countries. International agreements and co-operation have been necessary to reduce pollution of the river.

At the insistence of the Netherlands, which was concerned about increased salinity, France, Germany, Luxembourg, the Netherlands, and Switzerland began discussing arrangements for reducing pollution in the 1950s, and formed the International Commission for the Protection of the Rhine against Pollution (ICPRP) in 1963. This was a technical commission, charged with monitoring pollutants. To stem increasing pollution from industrial and municipal sources, the parties to the ICPRP signed the Convention for the Protection of the Rhine Against Chemical Pollution in 1976. In 1986 they agreed to the Rhine Action Programme, which seeks to produce drinkable water from the Rhine, reduce sediment pollution, and restore the Rhine environment so that

aquatic life returns. The ICPRP parties agreed to a 50% reduction (from 1985 levels) in the discharge of 30 priority pollutants into the river by 1995. France, Germany, the Netherlands and Switzerland agreed to share costs of $136 million. In the summer of 1991, the German chemical industry federation agreed to reduce the flow of toxic chemicals into the Rhine. These international efforts, combined with domestic pollution controls, have produced measurable benefits: since the early 1970s, concentrations of heavy metals have fallen and biological treatment of organic waste has reduced oxygen depletion and fish deaths.

However, so far, international agreements have failed to control some key pollutants; for example, nitrate concentrations (mostly of agricultural origin) continue to rise, and groundwater in Germany is increasingly contaminated with nitrate and pesticides. Salmon, at the top of the food chain and therefore a key indicator of river health, have disappeared completely from the Rhine. And although chloride was one of the pollutants originally targeted for control by the ICPRP, only one country, France, has reduced discharges.

The Great Lakes of America also have major pollution problems. Lake Erie is bordered by five states, each of which dumps untreated sewage, acid, oil, iron and other industrial waste into the lake; by the 1960s the fishing industry of Lake Erie had been destroyed by this pollution.

5.3.2 Groundwater

Pollution is not restricted to surface waters; groundwater can also be polluted. Aquifers rarely become polluted with organic wastes as these infiltrate into the ground only very slowly, and the wastes are broken down by biological action in the soil and rock. However, inorganic pollutants such as toxic metals and plant nutrients infiltrate easily, and once in an aquifer are difficult to remove because flow rates are low and residence times are long, so the effects of this type of pollution may continue for a long time.

5.4 Water treatment

Standards are necessary for water quality. The quality required depends on the intended use; drinking water, for example, needs quality standards different from those for industrial or irrigation water. The World Health Organization (WHO) has set water quality standards for drinking water and so has the EU (Table 8). In England and Wales the public water supply has to meet the Water Supply (Water Quality) Regulations of the 1989 Water Act, which incorporates all the EU standards.

Table 8 World Health Organization international drinking water standards and European Union drinking water standards

Substance or characteristic	Guide concentration/mg l^{-1}		Maximum acceptable concentration/mg l^{-1}	
	WHO	EU	WHO	EU
ammonia	–	0.05	–	0.5
cadmium	–	–	0.01	0.005
calcium	75	100	200	–
chloride	200	25	600	200
cyanide	–	–	0.2	0.05
fluoride	–	–	1.5	0.7–1.5
iron	0.3	0.11	1	0.3
lead	–	–	0.05	0.05
magnesium	50	30	150	50
nitrate	50	25	100	50
pesticides	–	–	–	0.0005
sulphate	200	25	400	250
TDS	500	–	1500	1500
pH range	7.0–8.5	6.5–8.5	6.5–9.2	6.0–9.5
BOD	0	0	0	0

The full standards include many other substances not listed here.

⬤ Do the groundwaters in Figure 51 fall within the WHO water quality standards for drinking water?

⬤ Yes, they both do.

The quality of the water required for industrial processes depends on the process so there is no general set of standards for industrial water equivalent to the standards for drinking water. High-pressure boilers require water of the highest quality, with more rigorous standards than for drinking water, whereas low-quality water, such as seawater, is usually adequate for cooling.

There are also no general standards for irrigation water; but there are three main quality criteria, involving the TDS, the sodium concentration, and the concentration of toxic substances.

(a) The maximum TDS of water that can be used for irrigation is usually 3000 mg l^{-1}, but this is not a precise limit, as different crops have different salt tolerances. Few fruit trees, for example, will tolerate much salt (2500 mg l^{-1} is usually the limit), vegetables and most cereals have a moderate salt tolerance (3500 mg l^{-1}), and grasses, cotton and date palms a high tolerance (6000 mg l^{-1}).

(b) Water with a higher sodium concentration than the combined calcium and magnesium concentrations is also generally unsuitable as it may damage the soil structure. If sodium ions replace calcium and magnesium ions in the soil, the permeability is reduced and the soil will be sticky when wet and very hard when dry.

(c) Toxic substances, if present in more than very small quantities in irrigation water, will prevent plant growth. For example, a concentration of more than about 1 mg l^{-1} of the element boron will affect growth.

Activity 8

This Activity looks at the chemical composition of bottled drinking water. Bottled waters are often described on the label as mineral waters, a scientifically inappropriate term, as the scientific meaning of mineral water is high-TDS groundwater, which would not be suitable for drinking. Bottled water is perhaps surprisingly not subject to the EU drinking water standards.

(a) Examine the label of any bottled water you have at home (or visit a supermarket to examine the water) and write down the dissolved substances it contains, with their concentrations (EU regulations require bottled waters to give this on their labels).

(b) Compare your list with the EU drinking water standards in Table 8. Does your bottled water approach or exceed the EU guide or maximum acceptable concentrations for any dissolved substance?

(c) If your bottled water has a high concentration of one or more substances, try to work out why the water has these high concentrations (for example, water from a limestone area may have a high calcium concentration).

The quality of water can be improved by water treatment processes, and this may be necessary before a source of water can be used.

5.4.1 Water treatment processes

Metal screens are used to strain floating or suspended debris and the larger living organisms from surface waters. The water is then stored in a reservoir, so that sediments and some of the organic particles which escape the straining process settle on the bottom, and the bacteria (which are all too small to be removed by straining) gradually die. Other organic impurities, which can give a taste or odour to the water, are oxidized in the upper layers of the reservoir. Storage has the disadvantages that the reservoirs required use a lot of land, and algae may grow in the water because of a build-up of nitrates. Water sprays, rather like fountains, are often used to aerate the water, so that oxygen is dissolved from the air more rapidly and its concentration in the water is increased. Thus organic impurities can be oxidized to harmless substances, and some dissolved metal ions are oxidized to give insoluble salts that can then be filtered out of the water.

Even after straining and storage, raw water may contain considerable quantities of suspended matter. Most of this consists of colloidal matter (which is matter in between solution and particulate form, about 10^{-8} m in diameter, and has negative electric charges). The colloidal matter can be reduced by filtration; but if there is a considerable quantity of it, it is usually more economic to make it *flocculate* (the colloidal particles are neutralized, so they can coalesce into bigger particles and sink out of the water). Filtration through sand and gravel then removes any fine particles of suspended matter and small organisms (mostly less than about 6×10^{-5} m in diameter) that still remain. In addition, algae and bacteria develop on and below the surface of the sand, where they decompose organic matter in the water passing through and digest some of the nitrates, phosphates and carbon dioxide dissolved in it, thus further purifying the water.

The WHO standard guideline for the pH of water for domestic use is 7.0–8.5 (Table 7); this range was chosen because more acidic water might dissolve metal pipes in the distribution system and more alkaline water might leave salt deposits in the pipes. In Britain it is often necessary to add an alkali such as lime to water with too low a pH, especially to water from peaty upland areas. Excessive hardness of water is usually reduced (softened) by precipitation or by the exchange of ions brought about by adding appropriate chemicals, but is kept above the EU minimum for softened water of $150\,mg\,l^{-1}$ as calcium carbonate.

The final treated water should contain no pathogenic bacteria, so the water must be disinfected. This is usually done chemically, by adding chlorine or ozone. In Britain, disinfection has eliminated water-borne disease — the last outbreak of disease linked to water supply was typhoid in Croydon in 1937. Most developing countries, however, not only cannot afford to disinfect their water, but often have no piped water to disinfect outside the main towns. Every year, millions of people, particularly children, die of diarrhoea spread by contaminated water.

Groundwater seldom requires much treatment, mainly because aquifers are efficient natural filters; disinfection is usually enough. Surface water,

---

Nitrate in drinking water

In recent years the nitrate concentration in surface and groundwater in some areas of the UK has been increasing, and is now above the EU maximum acceptable concentration of $50\,mg\,l^{-1}$.

There is concern that human health may be affected if these high-nitrate waters are used for drinking water. When nitrate is absorbed into the body, it can be converted to nitrite (NO_2^-) by bacteria in the digestive system. Nitrite may have two damaging effects:

1 It can combine with haemoglobin in the blood and prevent blood from combining with oxygen. If this happens extensively it leads to a serious condition called methaeomoglobinaemia, which in young babies can be fatal (blue baby syndrome). This is, however, very rare in Britain (the last case was in the 1970s) and may be caused by bacterial infection instead of or as well as high-nitrate water.

2 Nitrite is converted into substances which may cause stomach cancer, although there is no clear link.

Evidence is accumulating that nitrate levels in drinking water can only produce these effects when there is also malnutrition, but nevertheless the increasing nitrate levels are still causing concern.

The main source of nitrate in drinking water is from the high levels of fertilizer used in intensive agriculture to obtain high cereal yields. Part of the nitrogen in the fertilizer is not taken up by the crop, and is dissolved in overland flow, or leached from the soil, or infiltrates into groundwater. Another major source is also agricultural, from the spreading of large quantities of manure or slurry on farmland from intensive stock-rearing. All the major intensively farmed areas are affected, particularly the cereal-growing areas of northern Europe and the US, and the stock-rearing parts of northern Europe (Brittany, the Netherlands and Denmark). A third source of nitrate is effluent discharges from some sewage works.

During the 1980s the drinking water in many parts of Britain, particularly in central and eastern England, had nitrate concentrations above the EU limit of $50\,mg\,l^{-1}$. There was pressure from the EU for Britain to reduce the nitrate concentration to below $50\,mg\,l^{-1}$ everywhere, much resisted by the British Government, mainly because of the cost of doing so: nitrate concentration cannot be reduced by standard water treatment methods. However, legal action in the EU court against the water companies by the environmental pressure group Friends of the Earth, and further EU pressure, made the British government agree to reduce high nitrate levels.

The problem was *how* to reduce nitrate levels. To do this by water treatment methods would require ion exchange or biological denitrification, both very expensive procedures. Instead other 'lateral' approaches are being used:

(a) Alternative sources of water — closing some boreholes and opening new, low-nitrate ones.

(b) Blending high-nitrate water with that from a low-nitrate source.

(c) Reducing the *inputs* of nitrate into water, by using government legislation to reduce the use of fertilizers, manure and slurry in designated areas, called Nitrate Sensitive Areas. Here farmers are advised on ways to reduce nitrate leaching from the soil and receive grants to change their farming operations to less intensive ones, such as switching from cereals to grassland.

however, presents more problems. Unpolluted river water may require only straining, storage, aeration, filtration and disinfection. However, if the source of raw water is a poorer quality river, these treatments may have to be repeated several times. Amsterdam, for example, has the misfortune to be at the downstream end of the Rhine. To make the polluted Rhine water palatable it is successively aerated, filtered, aerated, disinfected, aerated, filtered, stored, aerated, filtered, aerated and disinfected again. Although it may be safe to drink after all this treatment, it still occasionally tastes awful!

Question 23

Table 9 gives the chemical compositions of a natural water. Would the water in Table 9 be a suitable source of water for (a) an EU public water supply, and (b) irrigation?

The Amsterdam water is river water that has been used many times on its way to the sea, as is the water from the Thames used by London. The quality of such recycled water depends on the efficiency of the sewage treatment, and in the next Section we look at the processes involved.

5.5 Sewage treatment

Communities situated on coasts commonly discharge untreated sewage into the sea. This is an acceptable method of disposal if the outfall is far enough offshore, if currents do not bring the sewage back to land, and if the discharge is not too great. In these circumstances, the organic matter can be broken down by bacteria in the sea. Sea discharges are not always satisfactory, however: many of Britain's beaches, for example, breach the EU Directive on bathing water quality. To comply with the Directive it is planned that all major discharges will be treated at a sewage works before disposal into the sea.

In inland areas in industrialized countries, sewage is usually treated to reduce the amount of oxygen-consuming organic material before it is discharged into lakes or rivers. Sewage treatment aims to reduce biodegradable material and material in suspension, remove toxic materials and eliminate pathogenic bacteria. It converts sewage into a liquid **effluent**, mainly water, leaving behind a **sludge**. The effluent does not need to be of drinking water quality or even of the quality of the water already in the river or lake. The discharge of effluent to streams and rivers in Britain is controlled through a system of **discharge consents** by the NRA or River Purification Boards. These limit the total volume, BOD and suspended solid concentration. There is no fixed standard, as the character and use of rivers varies greatly; for example, if a small quantity of effluent is discharged into a river with a high capacity for self-purification, it may be harmless provided the substances are not toxic. Effluents from industry often have to conform to additional standards, which may include limits on water temperature or toxic substances.

5.5.1 Sewage treatment processes

The *primary* treatment of sewage is the mechanical removal of coarse and fine solid material. The sewage first passes through screens, which trap pieces of wood, rags, wire, etc. The extracted material is usually buried, but it may be burned. The sewage then flows slowly through grit tanks, where particles of sand or grit settle out. Fine particles still remain suspended in the sewage, so it is passed to large primary sedimentation tanks where most of

Table 9 Chemical compositions of a natural water from Yellowstone National Park, USA

	Concentration/mg l^{-1}
bicarbonate	50
calcium	5
chloride	4
iron	0.1
magnesium	1
potassium	4
silica	135
sodium	28
sulphate	8
TDS	242
pH	7.6

the remaining particles fall out of suspension to form a sludge. Primary treatment removes about 35% of pollutants. The liquid leaving the primary sedimentation tanks still contains very fine solids and dissolved matter, so secondary treatment is usually required.

In Britain, most sewage goes on to *secondary* treatment. This is a biological process, involving the oxidation of dissolved organic material by micro-organisms, to decompose the organic compounds, a process similar to the ones taking place in rivers, the soil, or filter beds in water treatment works. The process is speeded up by increasing the amount of oxygen available, which can be done by two possible methods:

1 *Percolating filters*   The liquid is sprayed slowly over beds of broken stones, gravel, coke or plastic, which provide a large surface area for oxidation, and the micro-organisms (mainly bacteria) living within the filter break down the organic matter. The liquid that collects at the base of the filter contains some waste products from the filter organisms. These are separated from the effluent in secondary sedimentation tanks, producing more sludge. Percolating filters need very little supervision, but take up a lot of land.

2 *The activated sludge process*   This is a more recent method of secondary treatment. A sludge containing bacteria and other organisms is mixed with the liquid, and the whole mixture is agitated by paddles or has compressed air bubbled through it, to keep it well oxygenated. This process lasts about 10 hours, after which the mixture is allowed to flow to sedimentation tanks where the sludge settles out from the effluent.

Secondary treatment in addition to primary treatment removes about 85% of the pollutants, so that the effluent is usually sufficiently purified to be discharged to a river, lake or the sea. However, primary (physical) and secondary (biological) treatment remove only 30% of the phosphorus, 50% of the nitrogen and around 70% of toxic compounds, so if it is necessary to reduce plant nutrients or toxic compounds beyond these levels another method of treatment is required. This can be done — the plants are called advanced sewage treatment plants, but they are very expensive both to build and to operate.

5.5.2 Sludge disposal

What to do with the remaining sludge is more of a problem. Sludge is a nasty smelling, thick liquid, about 96% water, and sewage treatment plants have to dispose of vast quantities of it — a large plant will produce over a thousand tonnes each day. Before final disposal, sludge is sometimes held in closed tanks, where in the absence of oxygen, anaerobic bacteria further decompose the organic material, producing a relatively inoffensive digested sludge. The process takes 20 to 30 days at a temperature of around 30 °C. The gases methane and carbon dioxide are produced, and the methane can be used as a fuel to heat the tanks or to generate electricity for the treatment works.

Of the sewage sludge (including digested sludge) produced by sewage works in the UK in 1991, 26% was dumped at sea, another 47% was used on agricultural land, and most of the remainder was deposited in landfills or incinerated. Dumping sludge at sea needs to be carefully controlled, as the sea, like rivers and lakes, has only a limited capacity to absorb pollutants. It is particularly important to control pollution in enclosed seas such as the North Sea or the Mediterranean, where there is little water interchange with the larger oceans. Following pressure from other North Sea states, in 1990 the UK agreed to end dumping in the North Sea by 1998. Sludge disposed of on agricultural land is useful as a fertilizer and soil conditioner, and this is a more convenient method of sludge disposal for sewage works that are not on the coast. Tankers are used to transport the large volumes of sludge to the farms. But too much sludge is produced for all of it to be disposed of in this way—and not all sludge is suitable. For example, sludge containing toxic waste cannot be spread on fields. Instead it is dumped in natural or artificial depressions in the ground where it dries and decomposes slowly (and may cause unpleasant smells), or in trenches with a layer of soil on top, or it may be incinerated.

5.5.3 *The global dimension*

So far, we have considered sewage from a basically British perspective, where treatment is fairly routine. However, this is very different on a global scale. In Europe about 72% of sewage is treated, but in developing countries the figure is less than 5%; most of the urban sewage is discharged into surface waters without any form of treatment. Many cities in developing countries even lack sewer systems, let alone treatment plants. Sewage is often drained into rivers or lakes that may also be used as water sources— with obvious problems to health. For many developing countries, contaminated water containing bacteria, parasites and viruses derived from sewage are a major cause of death.

5.6 *Summary of Section 5*

1 Pollution is a deterioration of water quality caused by human agencies that makes the water less suitable for use than it was originally. Water does not have to be completely pure to be considered unpolluted.

2 Natural waters are not completely pure . Rainwater contains dissolved salts in relative proportions similar to those in seawater, but over a thousand times less concentrated. Rainwater has a greater relative proportion of dissolved gases, particularly carbon dioxide, than seawater, and this makes it slightly acidic. Surface water has a composition different from both rainwater and seawater; river water has a greater concentration of dissolved solids (TDS) than rainwater, and may contain suspended solids. Groundwater usually has slightly greater TDS values than surface water, and varies in composition, depending on the rocks through which it has passed. The TDS value of a groundwater depends on the length of time the water has been in contact with the rock, so the slowly moving, deeper groundwater has a higher TDS value.

3 Pollution can come from many different sources, including domestic sewage, farms, industry, mining, quarrying and cooling. There are many types of pollutants, including natural organic materials, living organisms, plant nutrients and toxic substances.

4 Water often has to be treated before it is of suitable quality for use. The quality needed depends on the use to which the water is to be put; quality standards for public water supplies are set by the WHO, the EU and some individual countries; but the quality required for industrial water and irrigation water can vary. The main water treatment methods used are straining, storage, aeration, flocculation, filtration and disinfection.

5 Sewage treatment aims to reduce the amount of organic and suspended solid material present, remove toxic materials and eliminate pathogenic bacteria, mainly by settlement or biological processes. The effluent is discharged into rivers, lakes or the sea, and the remaining sludge may be dumped at sea, disposed of on agricultural land, dumped in holes in the ground or incinerated.

Question 24

Which of the statements A–F should apply to a water used for public water supplies, if it is to meet WHO standards?

A   It will not be a risk to health.

B   It will not contain any polluting substances.

C   It will not contain any suspended solids or toxic substances, and will not have a BOD greater than zero.

D   It should have a nitrate concentration of less than $50\,\mathrm{mg\,l^{-1}}$.

E   It should contain no pathogenic bacteria.

F   It should have at least $1.5\,\mathrm{mg\,l^{-1}}$ of fluoride.

Activity 9

At the beginning of this Block I stated that water is probably the most important physical resource that we use. We often take its presence for granted in the UK: for most of us it arrives painlessly in our home out of a tap and we easily dispose of it by pouring or flushing it away. However, how much do you really know about your own water supply and sewage disposal? Are you drinking groundwater or river water? Is it recycled? What is its quality? Where does your sewage go? How much does it cost you? This Activity considers these questions. You may not be able to answer some of the questions without contacting your water company: this will take more time and effort than for most of the other Activities in the Course, and it is up to you whether you are interested enough to do it. Anyway, start the Activity and go as far as you want to.

(a) Do you have a piped water supply? (1% or so of homes in Britain do not: are you part of the 1%?)

(b) What is the source, or sources of your water? (Does it come from a reservoir, river, groundwater or a combination?)

(c) Where is your local water treatment works and what processes does it use?

(d) What is the chemical analysis of your water? Are there any particularly high concentrations, over or near EU limits?

(e) Do you have a water meter?

(f) What was the cost per person for water supply to your home last year?

(g) Is your home connected to sewers, or do you have a septic tank or cess pit?

(h) If your home is connected to sewers, where is your local sewage works and what processes take place there?

(i) How does the sewage works dispose of the effluent (into which river, lake, or the sea) and the sludge (sea, farmland, landfill or incineration)?

(j) What was the cost per person for sewage disposal from your home last year?

6 WATER RESOURCES FOR NOTTINGHAM AND JORDAN

In this Section we use the principles from Sections 1–5 to look at two contrasting case studies on water resources. Section 6.1 deals with the water supply for Nottingham, an industrial city in a developed country. The water supply for Jordan, a mainly arid, developing country where water resource problems are very different, is studied in Section 6.2.

The two video programmes Water for a City: Nottingham (Band 6) and Water for Jordan (Band 7) form important parts of the case studies, illustrating many of the points made in these Sections. The best time to study the video programmes is after completing each Section, but if you have time you may also wish to look at them before reading the text.

6.1 Water in Nottingham

Nottingham is the largest city in the East Midlands, with a population of just over a quarter of a million. It is an industrial city: it was a lace-making centre in the last century and now has a wider variety of industry, ranging from pharmaceuticals to tobacco products and bicycles. The demand for water in the Nottingham district, which includes south Nottinghamshire as well as the city, supplying a population of 692 000, averages 195 million litres per day.

The water used in Nottingham comes from three sources: the River Derwent, the Derwent Valley reservoirs (via the Derwent aqueduct) and the Sherwood Sandstone aquifer (Figure 54). The river supplies 42% of the total water used, reservoirs provide 17%, and groundwater forms the remaining 41%.

6.1.1 The River Trent

The River Trent, which flows through Nottingham, is the third largest river in Britain (after the Thames and the Severn) but its water is too polluted for use as the public water supply. Most of the river, including the Nottingham stretch, has a quality classification of 2 (Section 5.3); that is, it would be suitable for public water supply only after considerable treatment. Part of the river water is low-grade water (class 3) suitable only for certain industrial uses, and one of its tributaries, the River Tame, reaches class 4 (badly polluted). Most of the pollution is caused by sewage from the Midlands towns. In summer, when the natural discharge is least, up to half the water in the Trent at Nottingham may be sewage effluent. But the river is not as polluted as it used to be: as late as the mid-1970s over half the river was class 3 or 4. The improvement is mainly due to more efficient sewage treatment.

Figure 55 shows the average concentrations of ammonia in the Trent for 1968–70. Ammonia is produced by the breakdown of natural organic matter under anaerobic conditions (Section 5.2), and is therefore a good indicator of water quality.

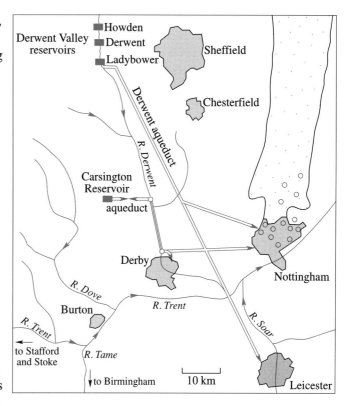

Figure 54 The water supply to Nottingham. Reservoirs are shown by blue rectangles, and groundwater pumping stations supplying Nottingham by blue circles. Aqueducts are shown by double blue lines. The lightly stippled areas indicate approximately where the Sherwood Sandstone outcrops near Nottingham.

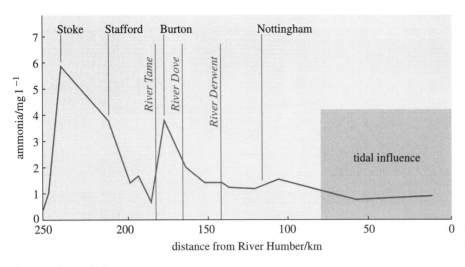

Figure 55 Water quality in the River Trent, 1968–70.

Question 25

Consider Figure 55.

(a) Was the ammonia concentration in the Trent at Nottingham higher or lower than the EU maximum for drinking water (Table 8, Section 5.4)?

(b) What is the probable cause of the large increase in ammonia in the Trent at Stoke?

(c) Do (i) the River Tame (which flows through Birmingham), and (ii) the Rivers Dove and Derwent (which flow through Pennine areas) improve or degrade the quality of the Trent?

Industry also adds to the pollution of the river. The potteries around Stoke contribute clay; engineering works add toxic substances; organic waste comes from sugar beet factories and brewing in Burton; and the coalfields in the Trent catchment area discharge acid and saline waters together with suspended solids into the river. Although it is poor quality, the Trent water does have one important use. About a third of Britain's electricity is generated by power stations along the banks of the Trent (it has been called 'Megawatt Valley') and large amounts of the low-quality river water are used for cooling.

As the Trent is too polluted for a public water supply, another river is used to supply most of Nottingham's water — the Derwent, which flows into the Trent about 10 km upriver of Nottingham (Figure 54). The following two subsections discuss how water is abstracted from the Derwent in two ways: from reservoirs in the higher parts of the Derwent Valley and directly from the river nearer to Nottingham.

6.1.2 Water from upland reservoirs

About 17% of Nottingham's water supply comes from three upland reservoirs 70 km to the north-west of the city in the Derwent Valley (Figure 54). Water from these reservoirs is transported to Nottingham through a pipeline, called the Derwent Valley aqueduct. The reservoirs are in the Peak District, where the catchment is moorland which has been partly forested. The catchment area is 95 km^2 and the average precipitation is 1356 mm per year. Table 10 gives details of the three reservoirs.

Figures 56 and 57 show the geology of the area. The rocks are of Carboniferous age, mainly Millstone Grit (hard, well-cemented, angular coarse-grained sandstones) and shales. The beds are nearly horizontal, dipping only gently to the east. We will use the information in Table 10 and Figures 56 and 57 to examine why the reservoirs were located in this area, why the dams are sited where they are, and the problems associated with the reservoirs.

Table 10 Derwent Valley reservoirs

	Howden reservoir	Derwent reservoir	Ladybower reservoir
commissioning date	1912	1916	1945
reservoir volume/10^6 m^3	9	10	29
greatest water depth/m	36	35	41
dam length/m	328	337	380
dam type	gravity	gravity	gravity
dam construction material	masonry^a	masonry^b	earth^c

a,b 1.25 million tonnes of Millstone Grit in total.

c 1 million tonnes of earth, and 0.1 million tonnes each of clay and concrete.

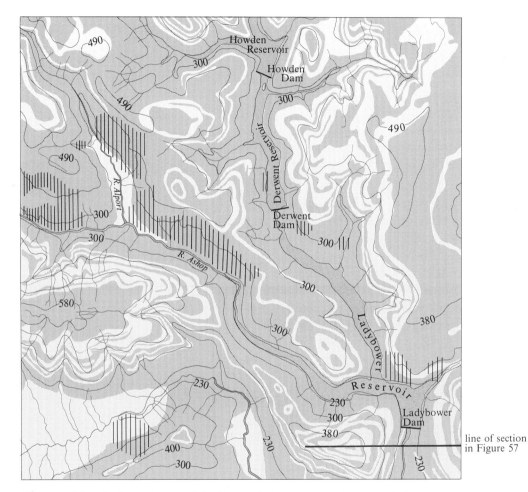

Figure 56 Geological map of the Derwent Valley reservoirs area. Shales are shown in light grey, grits in dark grey, and landslip areas by vertical black lines. The thin black lines are topographic contours, in metres. The area shown is 9 km across (i.e. from west to east).

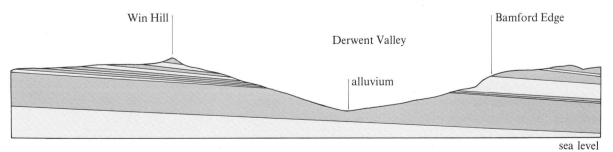

Figure 57 Geological cross-section along the east–west line marked on Figure 56. Shales are shown in light grey, grits in dark grey. The horizontal and vertical scales are the same in this Figure, but are three times the scale in Figure 56.

● How suitable is the area for reservoirs in terms of the availability of water?

○ The precipitation is quite high (1356 mm per year) and most of this will form overland flow. Infiltration is low because the rocks in the area — the grits and shales — are relatively impermeable. So there is a good supply of water. The area is also suitable for reservoirs as the Peak District is topographically higher than Nottingham, so water can flow through the Derwent Valley aqueduct to Nottingham under gravity.

From the information we have here, it is more difficult to assess what effects the reservoirs have had on the ecology and environment of the area. The few villages in the area were located on the flatter ground in the valleys, so building the reservoirs meant flooding these villages, and remains of the villages can still be seen when the water level is low. Apart from the protests of the villagers, there seems to have been little opposition to the building of reservoirs in the Derwent Valley; the powerful environmental and ecological pressure groups of today did not exist when these reservoirs were planned at the beginning of the century and in the 1930s.

● What geological factors had to be taken into account when considering whether reservoirs built in the area would be watertight?

○ The permeability and geological structure of the underlying rocks. Shale is impermeable and the grits, being hard and well cemented, have a reasonably low permeability, so there should be little leakage through the rocks themselves. However, the rocks have some secondary permeability along bedding planes and vertical fractures. There are also some faults in the area, which again could lead to loss of water; a fault crosses the Derwent Valley a few hundred metres downstream of Howden Dam, and detailed geological mapping of the area identified other faults.

● Would the geology of the area (Figures 56 and 57) have suggested any hazards due to instability of the rocks?

○ The rock layers are almost horizontal, so there should be little chance of landslides from slippage of grit along the shale bands into the reservoir (Section 4.3.2). However, there are areas where landslips have occurred — on the west side of Derwent reservoir and the north-east side of Ladybower reservoir.

● What would have been the two main considerations when planning the dam sites and choosing constructional materials for the dams?

○ A dam must be safe, and economic to build.

The valley floor is alluvium (a silt-size sediment deposited by the river), and this would need to be removed, to enable a stable foundation to be built into the rock below. The most economic dam sites are where valleys are narrowest, but this valley is more or less the same width, about 350 m, all along its length (Figure 56).

The first two dams to be built, Howden and Derwent Dams, were masonry dams, constructed from blocks of local gritstone (Table 10). Ladybower reservoir needed to be much larger than Howden or Derwent, and the dam was planned to be downstream of the point where a side valley entered the Derwent Valley, so that both valleys could be used as a reservoir although only one dam would need to be built (Figure 56). Ladybower Dam had to be longer and higher than the other Derwent Valley dams, so it was more economic to build an earth dam (Table 10). The dams all have cutoff curtains to prevent water seeping underneath the dam and weakening the foundations.

The Derwent Valley reservoirs trap water that would otherwise have flowed into the River Derwent, so a small quantity is released into the river from Ladybower reservoir to maintain the flow. Figure 58 is a hydrograph of the River Derwent just below the reservoirs.

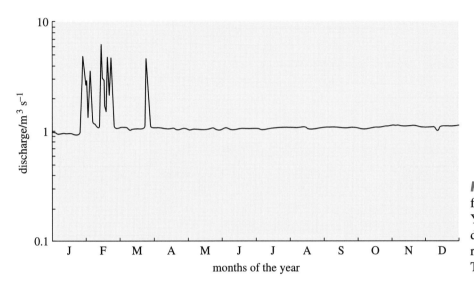

Figure 58 A hydrograph for the River Derwent at Yorkshire Bridge, immediately downstream from Ladybower reservoir, for the year 1971. The vertical scale is logarithmic.

Question 26

Consider Figure 58.

(a) How does this hydrograph differ from normal annual river hydrographs in Britain, such as Figure 42?

(b) What is the average daily discharge of water from Ladybower reservoir into the River Derwent?

(c) Why are there peaks in the hydrograph, showing discharges reaching $6.4\,m^3\,s^{-1}$ in January, February and March?

Figure 58 illustrates how reservoirs can be used for flood control. Ladybower reservoir usually catches the overland flow from the surrounding area and also the overflow from the Howden and Derwent Reservoirs, preventing large quantities of water flooding the Derwent Valley. It is only occasionally, when the reservoir is full, that flood water overflows down the valley, giving the winter peaks on the hydrograph. As Ladybower Dam is an earth dam (Table 10), water cannot be allowed to flow over its crest, as this would erode the downstream slope of the dam. Instead, surplus water goes into funnel-shaped overflows sited within the reservoir and is carried away through tunnels passing beneath the dam.

Although the River Derwent will only have a regulated quantity of water immediately downstream from the Derwent Valley reservoirs (except for occasional flood water), further down the river the regulated characteristics are lost as the river collects a lot more water from tributaries. Downstream river hydrographs therefore show a typical seasonal variation, with a high winter and a low summer discharge.

6.1.3 Water from the River Derwent

In the late 1960s the Trent River Authority, responsible for water resources in the east Midlands at the time, proposed a new reservoir at Carsington (Figure 54). This would be used as a river regulation reservoir to regulate the River Derwent, storing water during the winter months and releasing it back to the river as necessary during the summer. This means that water could be abstracted for use from the River Derwent further downstream, near to Nottingham, all year round. The reservoir was to be sited 10 km to the west of the Derwent Valley as no suitable sites in the valley itself were available. The river regulation principle would be used as it was cheaper and less disruptive to abstract the water from the river *near* Nottingham than to build long aqueducts from the reservoir to take the water directly to Nottingham.

The proposed reservoir, with an earth gravity dam, would have a capacity of 35 million cubic metres, and could supply up to 206 million litres per day — enough water for Nottingham's needs with some left over for Derby and Leicester. A reservoir at Carsington would only have a small catchment area and would not fill naturally, so it would have to be a pumped storage reservoir, pumping water to it from the River Derwent in the winter months when the river is full. The reservoir would be higher than the river, so water could be released back to the river in summer without pumping, by gravity flow. Pumping costs would be high, but could be reduced by using off-peak electricity at night.

In deciding which type of reservoir to build, and where, Trent River Authority had to take into account not only the cost, but also whether planning permission would be granted for the reservoir. A reservoir site at Carsington had the advantage that it was outside the Peak District National Park (unlike the Derwent Valley reservoirs), which had the effect of reducing environmental opposition to the scheme. Nevertheless, it took several public inquiries before the reservoir was finally approved in 1979 — over ten years after it had first been proposed. Carsington reservoir should have been completed in 1986, at an estimated cost of £36 million. However, in 1984 part of the nearly complete dam collapsed. A different design for the dam was proposed; reconstruction started in 1989 and was finished in 1991. The final cost of the scheme turned out to be £107 million! (See Section 6.1.5 on water cost.)

What made the Trent River Authority decide to build a reservoir at Carsington instead of looking elsewhere to increase their water resources? We have already seen that no more water could be extracted from the Derwent in summer without further regulation, and we shall see that no more water than at present can be supplied by the local groundwater. But while the Carsington reservoir inquiries were proceeding, the possibility arose of using surplus water from outside the region, such as from Rutland Water, which was then being built only 50 km to the south-east of Nottingham, though within the Anglian Water region. Rutland Water was completed in 1979, and is not fully used by Anglian Water; there will be spare capacity for some years to come. The Severn Trent Water Authority (the body responsible for water supply at that time) rejected the idea of using this water because Anglian Water offered the water at a price that included an allowance towards the capital costs of building the reservoir, that is, at the same price as its own consumers have to pay. The Severn Trent Water Authority decided that it would be cheaper to build its own reservoir rather than import this high-cost water from Rutland. Given the enormous final cost of the Carsington scheme, in retrospect it might have been cheaper to buy water from Rutland.

6.1.4 Groundwater

Nottingham is built on a sandstone aquifer of Triassic age, the Sherwood Sandstone. This sandstone varies in grain size, being fine-grained towards the base of the sequence, and coarse-grained with pebbles higher in the sequence.

⬤ What is the sorting, roundness and extent of cementation in the sample of Sherwood Sandstone shown in Plate 30? (You may need to refer back to Figures 13 and 25 for comparison.) Estimate the porosity of this sample of sandstone.

⬤ The sandstone is fairly well sorted, as most of the sand grains are about 0.5 mm in size. The grains are moderately rounded. It is poorly cemented, as most of the intergranular areas are blue, indicating that these are holes, not cement. The porosity of the sandstone is about 25–30%.

The Sherwood Sandstone is generally well sorted and poorly cemented, which gives it porosities of 15–30%. The hydraulic conductivity is 0.04–10 m a day, with the higher values being caused by secondary permeability along fissures.

⬤ By comparison with the porosity and hydraulic conductivity values in Table 5 (Section 3.5.1), how good an aquifer would you expect the Sherwood Sandstone to be?

⬤ A very good aquifer. The porosity and hydraulic conductivity (and hence the permeability) are around the highest that could be expected for a consolidated sedimentary rock, although not as high as those of some unconsolidated sediments.

Nitrate in Nottingham's groundwater

The concentration of nitrate in groundwater in parts of Nottinghamshire has been increasing, to levels where some boreholes are producing water above the EU nitrate limit for drinking water. This has been caused by the greater use of nitrate fertilizers in intensive farming.

Nitrate levels in groundwater are high *only* where the aquifer is unconfined, as here surface water which has dissolved nitrate from the soil can percolate down to the water table. Where the aquifer is confined below an impermeable layer of clay, the aquifer is protected from surface water infiltration from above (Figure 59).

Severn Trent Water (the water service company for Nottinghamshire) is tackling the nitrate problem in a number of ways:

1 Supporting a change of agricultural practice to reduce nitrate pollution in designated Nitrate Sensitive Areas.

2 Developing new deeper boreholes on the confined aquifer.

3 Blending the high-nitrate water with low-nitrate water.

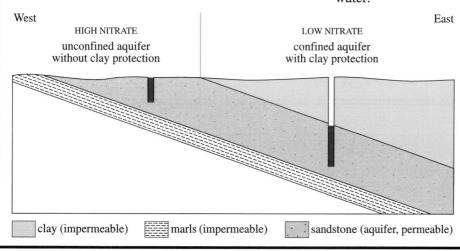

Figure 59
Cross-section of the Nottinghamshire Sherwood Sandstone aquifer. The aquifer is confined to the east under a layer of impermeable clay. Nitrate levels are rising where the aquifer is unconfined.

The Sherwood Sandstone is an extensive aquifer, and outcrops throughout much of Nottinghamshire (Figures 17 and 54). It dips to the east, extending underground as a confined aquifer below younger impermeable rocks to the east of its outcrop area. This aquifer initially supplied Nottingham with groundwater from boreholes within or near the city, but as the demand for water increased, the water table fell. More boreholes were drilled further from the city, to use parts of the aquifer where the water table was still near the surface, but the pumping gradually lowered the water table at these boreholes also.

The rate at which groundwater is extracted from the aquifer is now controlled so that the water table either does not fall any further or falls by only a small amount. Even so, much (41%) of Nottingham's public water supply comes from groundwater. It will not be possible to increase the present steady rate of extraction in the foreseeable future, though it will still be possible to increase the rate for short periods when necessary, as was done during the 1975–76 and 1988–92 droughts.

6.1.5 Water cost

The basic cost of supplying water for Nottingham depends on the source:

Derwent Valley reservoirs water	1.7p per cubic metre (a tonne)
River Derwent water	4.4p per cubic metre
Groundwater	3.1–4.7p per cubic metre

These are for 1992, and are *running costs*: they exclude the *capital costs* of building the reservoirs, aqueducts, treatment plants and mains, and also the charge for abstracting the water, paid to the NRA. The running costs are mainly made up of workforce, power for pumping and chemicals for water treatment. The reservoir water is cheapest, as it needs little or no pumping and not very much treatment. Groundwater costs are higher because although the water requires little treatment, a lot of energy is used in pumping the groundwater to the surface. River water is expensive because the water requires more treatment than that from the other two sources.

Question 27

What types of water treatment (Section 5.4) will be necessary for each of these three sources of water before the water is put into the public water supply?

The selling price of the water is about ten times the running cost, as it has to include capital costs, the charge made for abstraction, and, since privatization, a dividend for Severn Trent Water shareholders. A substantial part of the selling price of water from any recent project, such as the Carsington reservoir, includes repayment of the capital cost of the project. The capital

---

Capital repayment on the Carsington reservoir

The final capital cost of the Carsington reservoir scheme was £107 million, spread over the 25 years or so from the initial proposal, but with most incurred in the construction phase from 1979 to 1991. The capital cost might be planned to be recovered from water sales in about 10 years at a rate of £11 million a year.

The reservoir can supply a maximum of 35 million cubic metres a year, so the capital cost repayment contribution to water from Carsington would be a minimum of £11/35 per cubic metre, which is about 30p per cubic metre, about seven times the running costs for River Derwent water. In practice, the capital cost contribution will be even higher as it will have to include interest repayment on a loan or loss of income from the capital.

cost is incurred before any income from water sales can be made, and is often financed by a loan, repayable in a fixed number of years. This means that a project such as the Derwent Valley reservoirs, built between 1912 and 1945, will have had their capital costs repaid long ago, and so now provide a cheap source of water. The water from Carsington reservoir, however, is much more expensive as it must include repayment of the capital cost.

6.1.6 Future water supply

We have already seen that developing the last new source of water for Nottingham, Carsington reservoir, took about 25 years from first proposal to completion. Other major water supply projects have similar **lead times** — the time from recognition of the need to completion of the project — so *predictions* of future demand for water are essential, and must be made for around 25 years ahead.

Figure 60 is a long-term forecast of demand in the Nottingham district made by Severn Trent Water for the next 30 years. In making this, estimates were needed for the future population, per capita use, domestic demand, industrial, commercial and agricultural demand, and leakage.

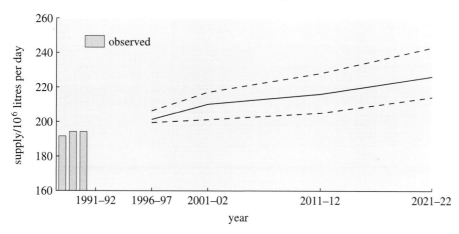

Figure 60 Long-term forecast of water demand for the Nottingham district, made in 1992. The solid line is the best estimate and the dashed lines are upper and lower bounds.

Question 28

Look at Figure 60. What is the overall increase in demand between 1991–92 and 2021–22 as a percentage of the 1991–92 supply?

Where will this extra water come from, and, indeed, can it be supplied at all? Severn Trent Water plan to meet the increased demand in two ways:

1 Increasing abstraction from the River Derwent, using Carsington reservoir to regulate the river to a greater extent. We have already seen that Carsington could supply 206 million litres per day to the Derwent, and although this is also used by parts of Derbyshire and Leicestershire, there is enough to increase the supply to Nottingham.

2 Reducing leakage of water in the distribution system. It has been estimated that about a quarter of the water put into the distribution system of aqueducts and mains in England is lost by leakage, although without metering of domestic supplies an accurate figure cannot be reached. Severn Trent Water alone has 38 500 km of water mains, so the proportion lost is perhaps not really surprising. The loss is not just in the form of spectacular bursts, but also in gradual undetected seepages from a distribution system built mainly during the last century.

Severn Trent Water estimated their leakage for the Nottingham district in 1992 as 22.9% (more than the predicted increase in demand in the next

30 years!). If these leaks could be repaired this would compensate for the increase in demand. But can it be done? Severn Trent Water aimed to reduce leakage during the next year (1993) to 22.0%. If they could make similar reductions each year this would supply the extra demand for the next 30 years without needing any new source of water. However, replacing or relining water mains is both very expensive and very disruptive, and part of the leakage occurs in private house, office or industrial distribution systems, over which Severn Trent Water have no control; so leakage is very unlikely to reduce by the 15% (to 7.9% total) needed to supply the extra demand in 30 years' time.

Now that you have studied the supply of water to Nottingham it would be a good time to view Video Band 6.

Video Band 6 Water for a City – Nottingham

Speakers

Sandy Smith and Geoff Brown   The Open University

The programme was made in 1983, updated in 1992. It studies:

1 the properties of the sandstone aquifer from which groundwater is extracted for Nottingham;

2 the structure of the dams and the geological location of reservoirs in the Derwent Valley and at Carsington;

3 treatment processes for the river water that supplies Nottingham;

4 sewage treatment processes that make it possible to return water to the River Trent after use.

The places shown in the programme can be located on Figure 54. Nottingham County Cricket ground and the caves in the sandstone aquifer are in Nottingham; the groundwater pumping station is about 15 km to the north of the city; the Derwent Valley reservoirs are in the Derwent Valley, 70 km to the north-west of Nottingham; Carsington reservoir is 10 km to the west of the Derwent Valley, the water treatment plant at Church Wilne is on the River Derwent downstream of Derby; Stoke Bardolph sewage works is by the River Trent on the east (the downstream) side of the city.

Important points made in the programme are:

(a) The Sherwood Sandstone (also called by the older name, the Bunter Sandstone, in the programme) is a good aquifer for two reasons: it has a fairly high porosity, as the sand grains are generally well rounded and poorly cemented; and it is fairly permeable, owing to primary permeability and also secondary permeability through cracks and fissures.

(b) There is a limit to the amount of groundwater that can be extracted from the Sherwood Sandstone (the safe yield). Boreholes cannot be too closely spaced, otherwise their cones of depression overlap, further lowering the water table.

(c) The location of the Derwent Valley reservoirs was selected mainly on the grounds of high precipitation in the area, fairly narrow valley sites for dams and low bedrock permeability. However, the geology is not perfect for reservoir construction because of the shale bands in the sandstone, which can lead to landslips. All three dams are gravity dams, i.e. they rely on their weight to resist the hydraulic pressure of the water in the reservoirs. The two older dams are constructed of masonry, from local sandstone, and the more recent, wider dam is an earth dam.

(d) The River Derwent just downstream of the reservoirs is a regulated river.

(e) The new reservoir for regulating the River Derwent was located outside the river valley, at Carsington, mainly for environmental reasons.

(f) The river water source for the public water supply of Nottingham is treated by coarse screening, storage in a reservoir, aeration, flocculation in reaction tanks, sand and carbon filtration, and disinfection by chlorination.

(g) Sewage from Nottingham is treated by settling, screening, primary sedimentation, and oxidation by the activated sludge method. The sludge is treated by anaerobic digestion and then used on farmland, and the effluent goes into the River Trent downstream of the city.

Question 29

The catchment area of the Derwent reservoir was increased in 1930 by diversion of water from the Rivers Ashop and Alport (Figure 56) into the reservoir. Why are the Ashop and Alport Valleys unsuitable sites for reservoirs?

6.2 Water in Jordan

Jordan is a Middle Eastern country, some $90\,000\,km^2$ in area (about two-thirds the size of England), and bordered by Syria, Iraq, Saudi Arabia and Israel. It has access to the sea only in the south, where it has a small length of coastline at the head of the Gulf of Aqaba. Jordan is not an affluent country and it has few physical resources; unlike some of its rich neighbours it has very little oil or gas. The main physical resources are phosphate and potash, used to make fertilizers. Agriculture is very important to the economy.

Topographically Jordan can be divided into three parts: the Rift Valley (containing the River Jordan and the Dead Sea); the highlands bordering the rift; and the desert plateau to the east. The Rift Valley is the surface expression of very large faults that extend northwards from the Gulf of Aqaba, through Jordan, to Lebanon and Syria (Figure 61). The highland area to the west of the

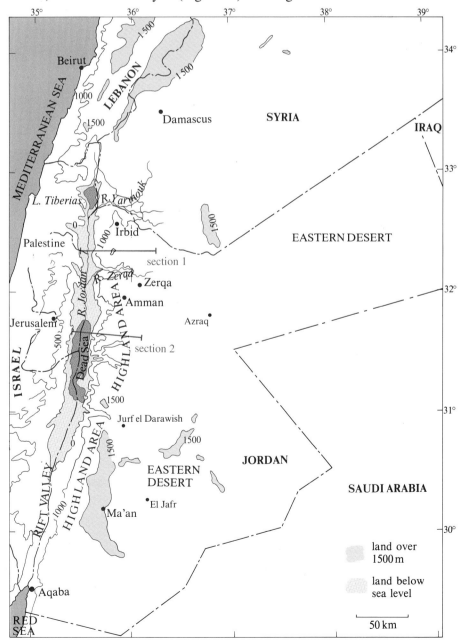

Figure 61 The topography and main towns of Jordan. The villages mentioned in the text are shown in small type. Topographic contours are in metres. Section 1 and Section 2 are the locations of cross-sections in Figure 65.

Rift Valley was under Israeli occupation from 1967 to 1994. The water resources of this area were unavailable and isolated from the rest of Jordan, so we shall not consider them in this study. The highlands to the east rise to a maximum height of 1727 m. To the east of the highlands is a high plateau (500–1000 m) known as the Eastern Desert (Figure 61, Plate 34).

Areas of the world where the precipitation is less than 200 mm a year and much less than the potential evapotranspiration are generally classed as **arid**. The precipitation in Jordan varies considerably, from 600 mm a year in the north-west to less than 50 mm a year in the south and east of the country (Figure 62). Most (91%) of Jordan has less than 200 mm a year of precipitation. This is very much lower than in the UK; over a half of Jordan has less than 50 mm, only about one-twentieth of the average annual precipitation of the UK. This is because there is no real equivalent in Jordan of the persistent wet, westerly winds that pick up moisture from the Atlantic Ocean and deposit it on the UK. Precipitation in Jordan occurs only when moist air from the Mediterranean area flows eastwards. This moist air is forced to rise over the highlands, which causes some precipitation (Section 2.2) on the highland area (Figure 62). Little moisture is left in this air after it has passed over the highlands, so very little rain falls to the east. As winds from other directions have already passed over land masses, they do not usually bring precipitation.

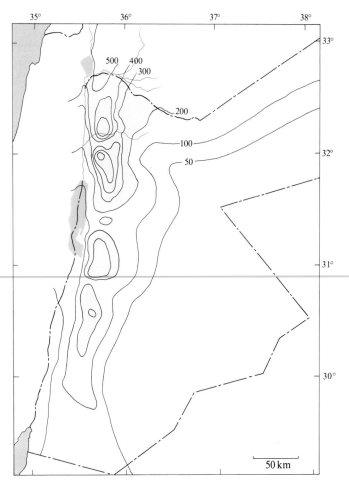

Figure 62 The average annual precipitation in Jordan, given in millimetres, for the years 1931–60. Most of the precipitation is rainfall, but there is some snow in the highlands. The areas with precipitation > 200 mm are shaded in light blue.

The potential evapotranspiration in Jordan reaches 3600 mm a year because temperatures are very high in the summer. This potential evapotranspiration is much greater than the rainfall, so most of the country (91%; where precipitation is less than 200 mm per year) is classed as arid. The precipitation is also irregular and unreliable; values for average precipitation have little practical meaning as the annual rainfall varies markedly (Figure 63).

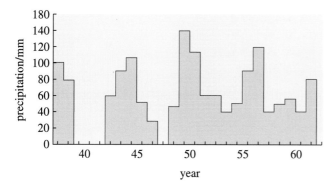

Figure 63 Annual rainfall at Jurf el Darawish (30° 42′ N, 35° 52′ E), at the western edge of the desert plateau in Jordan, for the years 1938–62. The average is 62 mm per year. No records are available for the years where no rainfall is shown.

● What is the maximum and minimum annual rainfall at Jurf el Darawish during the period covered by Figure 63? What is the maximum and minimum as a percentage of the average rainfall?

○ The maximum is about 144 mm per year, and the minimum about 28 mm per year. The average is given as 62 mm per year, so the maximum is about 232% and the minimum about 45% of the average rainfall.

This variation in annual precipitation is far greater than that in temperate climates. For instance, the annual rainfall during the drought of 1988–92 in Britain was still as much as 85% of the average.

The precipitation in Jordan is seasonal, occurring only during the winter months (October to April; Figure 64). This seasonal precipitation adds to the problems of water shortage in Jordan; the rain comes at the least useful time of year, as the greatest demand for water is during the very hot summer months.

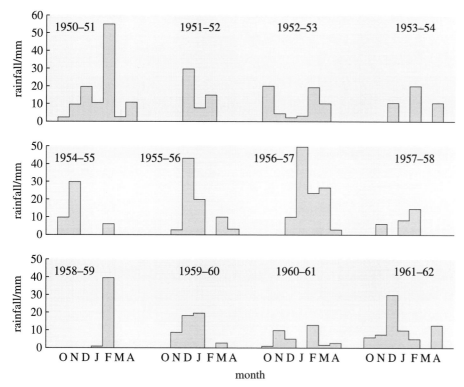

Figure 64 The distribution of rainfall from October to April (the winter months) at Jurf el Darawish, for the years 1950–62. No rain falls in other months (May to September).

Question 30

The area of Jordan is 90 000 km² and the average annual precipitation is about 100 mm. What is the total amount of water that falls on Jordan in an average year, in million cubic metres?

The answer to Question 30 may seem a large amount. However, the annual precipitation is highly variable, and the total amount ranges from 6200 million cubic metres in a dry year to 10 600 in a wet year. About 92% of this precipitation evaporates, leaving only about 8% of it for surface water and groundwater resources.

6.2.1 Uses of water

The population of Jordan is about three and a half million (1992), most of whom (91%) live in the northern highland area, with 51% in or around the capital, Amman, and the nearby town of Zerqa. The other centres of population are Ma'an in the southern highlands, and the port of Aqaba (Figure 61). Settlement patterns are heavily influenced by water availability. The Eastern Desert is only suitable for grazing by sheep, goats and camels, so is very sparsely populated, mainly by nomadic Bedouin (Plate 34).

About 20% of the water supply in Jordan goes to municipal use (domestic, office, small industry) and 5% to other industry but most, 75%, is used for agriculture which, because rainfall is low, seasonal and unreliable, is highly dependent on irrigation.

The main agricultural area is the Jordan River Valley (in the Rift Valley between the Dead Sea and Lake Tiberias; Figure 61), which has good soil and is warm all year round. Even in January the average daily temperature only falls to 15 °C, whereas in the highlands and Eastern Desert the temperature can drop to below freezing point in the winter months. Although it occupies only 0.6% of the country in area, the valley uses almost as much agricultural water as all the rest of the country owing to the requirements of intensive irrigation, and it could use more, if more were available. Agricultural produce from the Jordan Valley is the country's major export, so increasing the agricultural output (which would need more irrigation water) is a priority for Jordan.

6.2.2 Sources of water

Surface water

Most of the precipitation in Jordan occurs in the northern highland area (Figure 62). The total annual surface flow in Jordan originating from catchments within the country is only 480 million cubic metres. This is small compared with the volume of rain that falls (around 9000 million cubic metres) because most of it evaporates very quickly, leaving relatively small amounts of water for overland flow and infiltration. There are only three perennial rivers in Jordan: the Yarmouk in the north (which is shared with Syria and Israel), the Zerqa, and the Jordan (which was shared with Israel and now with Palestine). The Yarmouk and Zerqa are the only rivers that can be used for water supply. The Jordan is now a very small river, as much of the water that used to flow into it has been diverted into Israel and Palestine; also the quality of its water is poor. As well as the three rivers, there are seasonal flows of water in many wadis, which are valleys that have water flowing along them during the wet winter season but not during the summer. The Dead Sea (actually a lake) is no use as a water supply because it is even more saline than seawater.

To make the best use of surface runoff it should be stored during the wet winter season for use in the hot summer months. However, because of loss of water by evaporation, reservoirs are less efficient in hot climates.

Question 31

Suppose there is a reservoir in a wadi on the side of the Jordan Rift Valley that initially contains 2 million cubic metres of water, and that the surface of the reservoir is 500 m long by 200 m wide. The potential evapotranspiration is 3000 mm a year. How much water would be lost from the reservoir by evaporation in one year? Express your answer both in cubic metres and as a percentage of the volume of water initially contained in the reservoir.

This loss from evaporation may not seem very high, but it is many times higher than the loss would be from a similar reservoir in Britain. Loss from evaporation can be reduced by building deep reservoirs with small surface areas: for example, in a narrow, deep, river valley.

Groundwater

In parts of Jordan, groundwater is the *only* source of water, and in many areas it is the main source. It is difficult to assess groundwater resources in Jordan because information about the water tables, potentiometric surfaces, rates of flow and water quality is incomplete. There is also a difficulty in making separate assessments of groundwater and surface water resources because a large proportion of the surface discharge in the rivers and wadis is base flow, from groundwater (Section 4.2). In the summer, when there is no rain, almost all of the surface flow of rivers is base flow.

The geology of Jordan is illustrated by the cross-sections in Figure 65. The oldest rock group is the Precambrian basement, formed of igneous rocks, on top of which are Precambrian, Palaeozoic and Mesozoic sandstones, followed by Mesozoic and Tertiary sediments: limestone, dolomite ($CaMg(CO_3)_2$), marl (a calcareous mudstone) and chert (a siliceous sediment). The rocks generally dip at a low angle towards the east, but locally may also dip to the west into the faulted rift valley (Section 1 in Figure 65).

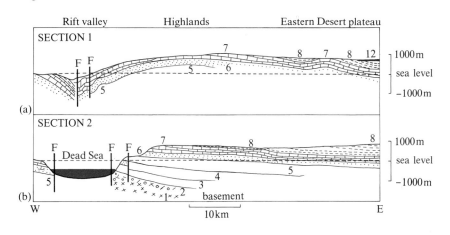

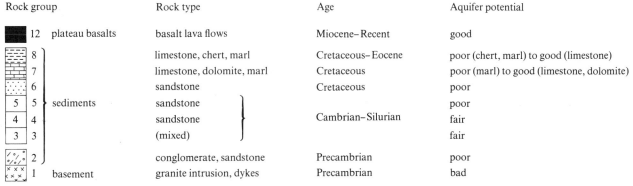

Figure 65 Geological cross-sections of part of Jordan. The locations of the sections are on Figure 61. The vertical scale is about four times the horizontal scale. F represents a fault.

Rock group			Rock type	Age	Aquifer potential
12	plateau basalts		basalt lava flows	Miocene–Recent	good
8			limestone, chert, marl	Cretaceous–Eocene	poor (chert, marl) to good (limestone)
7			limestone, dolomite, marl	Cretaceous	poor (marl) to good (limestone, dolomite)
6			sandstone	Cretaceous	poor
5	sediments		sandstone		poor
4			sandstone	Cambrian–Silurian	fair
3			(mixed)		fair
2			conglomerate, sandstone	Precambrian	poor
1	basement		granite intrusion, dykes	Precambrian	bad

The major aquifers in Jordan are the Cambrian–Silurian sandstone in the south of the country (Figure 65, rock groups 3 and 4), the Cretaceous–Eocene limestones and dolomites found in a number of places (Figure 65, rock groups 7 and 8), and the basalts in the north (Figure 65, rock group 12). These aquifers are recharged mainly in the highlands where the rainfall is relatively high. The groundwater in the aquifers flows in the direction of dip, which is generally to the east. This means that although precipitation over the Eastern Desert is very low and there is no water at the surface except during the rare rainstorms, there is always water underground. However, some of the groundwater in the aquifers flows west from the highlands to the rift valley. The basalt aquifers are recharged mainly in the north, in a highland area in Syria.

The safe yield of renewable groundwater resources in Jordan is estimated as 275 million cubic metres a year. Extracting more is possible, but because of the important contribution of base flow to surface waters this would lower water table levels and base flows, and so reduce surface flows: this would be exploitation above the safe yield.

As well as renewable groundwater, Jordan has non-renewable groundwater. This is groundwater which is being recharged very slowly or not at all. This water accumulated either by very slow recharge over a long time with little or no discharge, or by recharge during a period in the past when the climate was wetter. Not all of this water is suitable for use, as some has a high salinity. At present, this non-renewable groundwater is being used— it is mined to provide most of the water supply for Aqaba. In the mid-1970s the supply to Aqaba was only 2 million cubic metres a year, provided by wells in a nearby wadi. Aqaba has developed rapidly since then, both as a port and as a tourist and industrial centre. The increased water supply comes from wells in the Cambrian–Silurian aquifer (Figure 65) 50 km to the east. However, this water is believed to be of considerable age. Recharge of the aquifer today takes place mainly in Saudi Arabia, and is very slow. In general, groundwater mining can only be used either where the quantities of water required are small, such as the local desert irrigation schemes, or for a short time, because the resource is not renewable. It is estimated that the aquifer could provide 125 million cubic metres a year, but only for 50 years. Another aquifer further north near El Jafr could be mined to provide an additional 18 million cubic metres a year.

The total water resource of Jordan is given in Table 11. However, this ignores the rainfall variability, and, as we shall see in the next section, the demand for water.

Table 11 Water resource theoretically available on a sustainable basis and water supplied in Jordan in 1990 (quantities are in million cubic metres a year)

	Surface water	Renewable groundwater	Non-renewable groundwater (50 years supply only)
water theoretically available	480	275	143
water supplied 1990	360	330	190

6.2.3 Water supply

The water supplied in Jordan for 1990 is given in Table 11.

● What are the differences between the water supplied and that theoretically available?

○ Less surface water, but more renewable and non-renewable groundwater, is being supplied than is available on a long-term basis.

The amount of surface water used was lower because of drought in the region: the rivers did not supply the theoretically available amount given in Table 11. The groundwater use was above the safe yield of both the renewable and non-renewable resource: this high extraction rate has reduced the water quality, caused the abandonment of some wells, and reduced base-flow contributions to surface flow. But why is groundwater being extracted above its safe yield? This is because of the great demand for water in Jordan. Despite overexploitation of groundwater, the demand is still greater than the supply and more water would be used if it could be supplied. The water supply for Amman, for example, is cut off for parts of the day during the dry summer months. The supply figures are not the same as the demand, as they would usually be in Britain.

When we want water in Britain, we just turn on a tap; we assume that water will always be available. This is not generally true of Jordan. In the main towns there are taps in some houses (although water will not always come out of them); but in the desert, water is available only at widely spaced wells. Of course, the ease of availability of water has a great effect on the demand (Table 12): more is used where there is a piped water supply. In the desert, water is the resource of prime importance and it is used only at subsistence levels (Section 1.1). Just as each Bedouin tribe has always carefully guarded the right to use its wells, on a larger scale there are major international disagreements over water, such as those between Jordan, Syria and Israel over the River Yarmouk water. The disposal of water after use in Jordan is also often different from what happens in Britain, as sewage treatment exists only in the main towns.

Table 12 The daily demand for domestic water per person in Jordan in 1985 for the Amman area and in 1980 for the other areas (quantities are in litres per person per day)

Area	Quantity
Amman, Zerqa, Irbid	80
other towns and villages with piped water supply to standpipes and houses	65
areas with no piped water supply	35

Question 32

Taking the population of Jordan as 3.5 million and the total water supplied in 1990 as 880 million cubic metres (Table 11), what is the average use in litres per person per day? How does this compare with the value for England and Wales (Question 4)?

Figure 66 illustrates the yearly growth in the municipal water supply and also in the demand. Supply shortages occurred in the summers up to 1989, and all year round in 1990, the shortages increasing from 3 million cubic metres a year in 1986 to 13 million cubic metres a year in 1990. Municipal water rationing started in the Amman area in 1988. Some of the shortages in 1990 were caused by an unexpected population increase due to the return of Jordanians and refugees to the area as a result of the invasion of Kuwait.

Water in the Amman–Zerqa area comes mainly from wells in the wadi between the towns. There are two main aquifers, an upper, unconfined aquifer formed of alluvial deposits and Cretaceous–Eocene limestone (Figure 65, rock group 8), and a lower, confined aquifer of Cretaceous dolomitic limestone (Figure 65, rock group 7). The extraction may be above

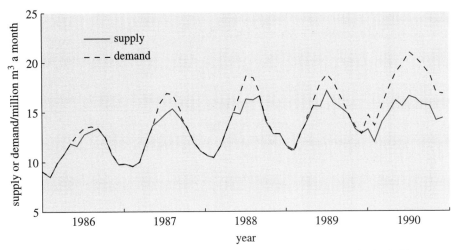

Figure 66 Monthly municipal water supply and demand for Jordan in 1986–90.

the safe yield, as the potentiometric surface in the lower aquifer is falling, but the rates at which the aquifers are recharged are not known accurately. Some of the sewage effluent from Amman is recharging the upper aquifer; this adds to the quantity of water available in the aquifer and prevents the water level falling, but leads to problems of water quality; in particular, nitrate levels are high.

Water is also piped to Amman from Azraq, a desert oasis 100 km to the east of Amman. Azraq is the focus of drainage of a number of wadis in a closed basin in the desert. Rainfall in this basin is low (about 50 to 200 mm per year) and the potential evapotranspiration is high (2000 to 2200 mm per year), but floods from occasional rainstorms bring an average of 5 million cubic metres of water a year into the basin. However, most of the water at Azraq comes from the basalt aquifer which feeds springs with 14 million cubic metres of water a year. The quality of this water is quite good: it has a TDS of about 200 mg l^{-1}.

The Irbid area is supplied mainly by groundwater from the same aquifers that supply Amman. The aquifers are deeper at Irbid, and the water is 150–300 m below the surface. Additional supplies are piped to Irbid from wells at desert sources. Irbid is close to the River Yarmouk, so a good way of increasing the water supply in future would be to build a reservoir on this river.

The Jordan Valley gets its water supply from the Yarmouk and Zerqa Rivers, and from surface water and wells in wadis on the side of the valley. There are reservoirs to trap winter floodwater on the River Zerqa and in some of the wadis, and there are plans to build additional dams. The discharge of the River Zerqa, an average of 88 million cubic metres a year, is almost as great as the combined flows in all the wadis, estimated as 107 million cubic metres a year. However, the discharge of the River Yarmouk at the point where it reaches the Jordan Valley is much greater, and much of the winter flood flow is wasted as there is no reservoir on the river to store it.

As water in the Jordan Valley is not plentiful, it has to be used very efficiently. Water from the rivers and wadis is fed into a concrete-lined canal which carries it along the valley, where a number of irrigation techniques are employed:

1   In surface-furrow irrigation, water flows under gravity along channels to the fields, and then along furrows (Plate 35). The efficiency of surface-furrow irrigation (i.e. the proportion of the water supplied that is used by the crops) is only about 50%, because evaporation and infiltration remove a lot of the water from the channels taking the water to the fields.

2   Water is also transported from the canal through pressurized pipes and then sprayed over the land (as with garden sprinklers). Spray irrigation is about 75% efficient.

3   Drip irrigation, where each plant is fed by an individual drip from a pipe, is up to 95% efficient, but more expensive to install. Plastic water pipes are used, with holes at set intervals, and one plant is planted at each hole. A plastic sheet is used to cover the ground around the plants, to prevent evaporation and weed growth. The ground between the holes is dry but each plant is adequately watered by its individual drip feed (Plate 36). The distance between the holes and the rate of drip are adjusted to suit the different crops.

Soil salinization in the Jordan Valley has been avoided by using large quantities of irrigation water to wash the salts through the soil, trapping the salty water in field drains and then channelling it into the Jordan River at the lowest part of the valley. However, this has degraded the quality of the Jordan, which is now too saline to be used for either water supply or irrigation.

Outside the Jordan Valley, where irrigation schemes are less extensive and less carefully planned, salts in the soil and water can be a problem. An example is at El Jafr, in the Eastern Desert 50 km east of Ma'an, which is one of the irrigation projects designed to encourage the Bedouin to settle in one place by providing enough water for irrigated agriculture. El Jafr, like Azraq, is at the focus of an inland drainage basin and has good alluvial soil. As it receives less than 50 mm of rain a year, rain-fed agriculture is not possible. However, just below the alluvium there is an aquifer 30 m thick which is recharged in the highlands to the west. Water is pumped from this aquifer and used for irrigation by the surface-furrow technique. Some of the irrigation water then infiltrates through the alluvium and back into the underlying aquifer, from where it can be pumped back to the surface for reuse. Enough water has been used to prevent salt buildup in the soil, but the recycling of the water has caused salt buildup in the aquifer water instead; the original groundwater had 600 to 1000 mg of dissolved salts per litre, but now it has up to 6000 mg l^{-1} and is too salty to use for drinking or irrigation (Section 5.4). One remedy would be to prevent the water from sinking back into the aquifer by installing drains under the fields to take the water away from the area. However, this would be expensive and would also reduce the recharge of the aquifer.

6.2.4 *Future water supply*

Obviously the main problem in Jordan is the shortage of water, but in addition the rainfall is unreliable and seasonal, sources of water are far from areas of demand, water quality is not always satisfactory, and municipal and agricultural interests are in competition.

The demand for water is rising rapidly due to a high rate of population growth (at 3.6%, in 1992, one of the highest in the world) and increasing development. The municipal demand, for example, is predicted to *double* between 1990 and 2010; compare this with the 15% rise predicted for the Nottingham district between 1991 and 2021.

It is unlikely that any new schemes within Jordan will be able to increase the water supply greatly, as water is already being used up to, and sometimes above, its safe yield. One possibility is to recycle the water. This would probably be of most use in the Amman–Zerqa area, where over half the domestic supply is returned to the hydrological cycle as sewage effluent, which joins the surface runoff or groundwater. This could be extracted further down the Amman–Zerqa valley and pumped back to Amman.

What would be a major drawback of this scheme?

 The major drawback would be the quality of the water to be recycled. At the moment only part of the sewage from Amman is treated, and although considerable natural purification takes places during the journey down the river valley (Section 5.2), there could be long-term risks to health.

An alternative approach for increasing the water supply to a large extent would be in schemes developed with neighbouring countries. Jordan shares some of its most important water resources (the River Yarmouk and the River Jordan) with other countries, and the allocation of water between each country is one of the most difficult regional issues. Each country has defended what it has regarded as its own water (at times violently), developing its own systems, and the region as a whole has failed to develop the most efficient, unified approach to manage water resources.

For example, a scheme that would solve many of Jordan's water problems is for a reservoir to be built on the River Yarmouk to store the seasonal floodwater. Part of this would be piped to Amman and Irbid, and the rest would be released to the Jordan Valley. Preliminary studies have been made but as yet no construction work has started. This would be a very large and expensive project; the reservoir would have a capacity of 388 million cubic metres (for comparison, Kielder Water, the largest reservoir in Britain, has a capacity of 190 million cubic metres), and even the feasibility study and detailed designs cost £7 million in the late 1970s. Building the reservoir may cost up to £1000 million. Ironically, the major problem is not the cost of the reservoir, but the fact that the River Yarmouk also flows through Syria and Palestine. No agreement between the three countries on how to allocate the water has so far been reached. Unless and until an agreement is signed, a reservoir cannot be built. The region is still an area of political tension, so a quick solution to this problem is unlikely.

Another possibility for increasing the water resources of Jordan was considered in the 1980s, and that is to set up a major water transfer scheme from another country. Iraq has two major rivers, the Euphrates and Tigris, and has a surplus of water. The proposed scheme entails transferring some 200 million cubic metres of water a year for a distance of about 650 km, from the Euphrates to Jordan. A feasibility study was carried out in 1983; a pipeline, pumping stations, a reservoir and power stations would have to be built, at a total cost of £500–800 million. However, since the Gulf War in 1990–91 it seems unlikely that this scheme will go ahead.

So what will happen to Jordan's water supply? Will water become increasingly rationed and development curtailed? This is a real possibility, unless Jordan reaches agreement with its neighbouring countries on a unified approach to water use, and/or restructures its own usage patterns to use water *sustainably*.

For example, Jordan uses 75% of its water for irrigated agriculture. If this were halved, by reducing land under irrigation and making irrigation even more efficient, the water saved could be used for less water-intensive industrial uses, which could contribute more to the economy than would be lost by reduction in agricultural exports. This economic transition would be a major change, and would be difficult — as farming is traditional and culturally embedded in the area — but possible. In the end, using water for irrigation where it is a scarce resource and when there are competing demands for water is an inappropriate use. Food is produced more efficiently in areas of sufficient rainfall or abundant irrigation water, and can be traded for other resources.

Now that you have studied the water resources of Jordan, it would be a good time to view Video Band 7.

Video Band 7   Water for Jordan

Speakers

Sandy Smith and Ian Gass   The Open University

The programme, which was made in 1983, studies:

1   The characteristics and problems of water resources in an arid area.

2   The underground water resources (hydrogeology) of Jordan.

3   The water supply in the Wadi Rumm area, 70 km south of Ma'an, where permeable sandstones lie unconformably on impermeable Precambrian crystalline rocks resulting in a spring-line along the unconformity.

4   The oasis at Azraq, in the Eastern Desert, supplied with water by an unconfined basalt aquifer.

5   A drilled flowing artesian well near Ma'an, in southern Jordan.

6   A desert agricultural scheme at El Jafr, southern Jordan, planned to encourage Bedouin settlement. Water is pumped to the surface from a shallow unconfined aquifer.

7   The hydrogeological characteristics of Wadi Wala, the valley shown on Figure 61 to the east of the Dead Sea just south of Section 2.

8   The Jordan Valley, the main agricultural area in Jordan, where irrigation water is used efficiently in sprinkler and drip irrigation techniques.

9   The use of water for the fertilizer industry.

The locations of these places are shown in Figure 61. The programme was filmed at a time when the country to the west of the River Jordan was Israel: it is now Palestine.

Important points made in the programme are:

(a) Precipitation in arid areas, as well as being low, is often seasonal and unreliable. Precipitation in Jordan occurs only in the winter.

(b) Groundwater is an important source of water in Jordan. The programme studied two aquifers in detail: the Nubian Sandstone in the south of the country, underlain unconformably by a Precambrian granite, and basalt lava flows in the north-east. Igneous rocks are not usually good aquifers, but the rubble at the bottom of a flow is fairly permeable. Water flows through these horizons south into Jordan from Syria.

(c) The rate of evaporation in Jordan is high, and this can lead to problems of salt buildup in unconfined aquifers.

(d) Water from flowing artesian wells can form oases in the desert, useful for watering nomadic animals. The confined aquifer supplying the artesian water is recharged in a mountainous area of high precipitation. Water in an artesian well will flow to the surface if the potentiometric surface of the confined aquifer is above ground level.

(e) Streams in Jordan are often seasonal, flowing only in the winter months in valleys called wadis. There may be surface water flowing in the lower parts of wadis during the summer, derived from stored groundwater; this is base flow.

(f) In Jordan it is essential to store water in reservoirs for use in the dry summer season. Waste must be kept to a minimum so the techniques of sprinkler and drip irrigation are often used, especially in the Jordan Valley, the main agricultural area.

(g) The main physical resources of Jordan, phosphates and potash, need water for their extraction and processing.

Question 33 _____

In Table 4 we saw that igneous rocks usually have a low porosity and permeability, and should therefore make bad aquifers. Why is the basalt lava flow a good aquifer?

6.3   Summary of Section 6

1   Nottingham uses water almost entirely for domestic and industrial purposes; very little is used for irrigation.

2   The water supply for Nottingham comes from river water (42%), reservoir water (17%) and groundwater (41%). The river water comes from the River Derwent, not from the River Trent which flows through

Nottingham, as the Trent is more polluted. Groundwater for Nottingham is from the Triassic Sherwood Sandstone aquifer, which has a porosity of 15–30% and a hydraulic conductivity of 0.04–10 m per day. The reservoirs that supply Nottingham with water are in the Derwent Valley, in the Peak District. There is a good supply of water there, and because it is higher than Nottingham the water is able to flow by gravity through a pipeline to Nottingham; another advantage is that the geology of the Derwent Valley (grits and shales) makes the reservoir area relatively watertight. The lead time for Carsington reservoir construction was about 25 years.

3   The basic running costs of water from the three sources are: river water 4.4p per cubic metre, reservoir water 1.7p, and groundwater 3.1p–4.7p. The groundwater requires little treatment, although it needs a lot of pumping, but the river water must be extensively treated.

4   Estimates of future demand from the Nottingham area predict that the demand will increase by about 15% between 1991–92 and 2021–22. The water supply will be increased using Carsington reservoir more fully to regulate the River Derwent, and by reducing the leakage in the distribution system.

5   In Jordan the precipitation is between less than 50 and 600 mm a year, but 91% of the country has less than 200 mm a year and a very high potential evapotranspiration, so it is classed as arid. Precipitation is unreliable and seasonal, occurring only during the winter months.

6   Approximately 75% of the water in Jordan is used for irrigated agriculture, mainly in the Jordan Valley, which has good soil and warm winters. The demand for both municipal and agricultural water in Jordan exceeds the supply: there are shortages and water rationing.

7   Jordan has only three perennial rivers, but many wadis which have a surface flow in the winter months only. The Dead Sea is more saline than seawater, so it cannot be used for water supply. The main aquifers in Jordan are Cambrian–Silurian sandstones in the south, Cretaceous–Eocene limestones and dolomites throughout the country and Miocene–Recent basalts in the north. The aquifers are recharged mainly in the highlands, except for the basalts, which are recharged mainly in Syria. This groundwater is renewable, but Jordan has other groundwater which is being recharged very slowly (if at all) and is therefore classed as a non-renewable resource. This can be mined for use, like other physical resources. At present (1994) Jordan is not only mining its non-renewable groundwater but also exploiting its renewable groundwater beyond the safe yield.

8   Demand for water in Jordan is rising rapidly, even though it is already in short supply. The supply could be increased to a small extent by municipal recycling, or a larger extent through unified water development schemes between Jordan and its neighbouring countries, although the latter seems politically unlikely at present. In the long term, Jordan must restructure its economy away from traditional irrigated agriculture towards sustainable water use.

Question 34

How does the average quantity of water used for domestic purposes differ in England and Jordan? Suggest reasons for this difference.

7 EXTENDING WATER RESOURCES

Existing supplies of water will have to be used in different ways, or new sources will have to be found, to satisfy a greater demand for water in the future. This Section looks at the alternative methods of exploiting water resources by water transfer, estuary storage, conjunctive use, and also at methods for creating new supplies of fresh water by desalination, rain-making and the use of icebergs.

7.1 Water transfer

There is often a surplus of water in one area and too little in another, both on a small scale within a country and on a larger, continental scale. One method of increasing the supply to the areas with too little water is by **water transfer** from areas with surplus water. For example, Birmingham, in the West Midlands, is supplied with water transferred from reservoirs in mid-Wales. The industrial cities of South Yorkshire are supplied with water from rivers to the north through the Yorkshire Grid Scheme, which uses rivers and large mains to transfer water from one river catchment area to another.

On a large scale, water is transferred between major river basins in the south-western USA by means of large canals, pumping stations and tunnels. An enormous quantity of water, around 5500 million cubic metres, is transferred each year 300 km or so from the Colorado River basin to California, where it is used mainly for irrigation in the agricultural areas of southern California, but also for public water supply in Los Angeles, San Diego and other cities. Half of all the water used in southern California comes from the Colorado, and California would like even more but the river is unable to supply it. It is interesting to compare the amount of water transferred to California with the total amount of public water supply in England and Wales (Table 2, Section 1.2); they are about the same, although the population of California is only about half that in England and Wales. Most of the California water, however, is used for irrigation, which is a minor factor in England and Wales.

Large-scale water transfer is a very expensive way of increasing water resources, but necessary when there are no alternative local sources. Two water transfer schemes even longer than the Euphrates scheme in the Middle East (Section 6.2.4) were proposed in the 1960s, both involving movement of water on a continent-wide scale. One was the North American Water and Power Alliance (NAWAPA; see the Box below). The second scheme was water transfer within the USSR, to divert water from Siberian rivers to the south, to provide more irrigation water for Central Asia. The Siberian rivers flow northwards into the Arctic Ocean and this scheme would involve damming rivers to create huge reservoirs and 'turning the rivers round' — i.e. making the water flow to the south.

Neither NAWAPA nor the USSR scheme was implemented nor looks likely to be in the future. The most obvious reason for this is the capital cost of the schemes, due to the massive engineering works involved in diverting water on a continental scale. The value of the water, especially if used for irrigation, is insufficient to repay or justify the construction cost. The second reason, which applies to both the North American scheme and now for the individual republics of the former USSR, is the difficulty of

The Snowy Mountains scheme

A large water transfer system is the Snowy Mountains scheme in New South Wales, Australia. Rainfall on the Snowy Mountains flows away to the east, which has sufficient water, and to the west, where there is a shortage of water because of very low rainfall and water use in irrigation for agriculture. The scheme traps part of the flow of the Snowy and Murrumbidgee Rivers on the east side of the mountains in reservoirs (Figure 67). This water is then pumped through tunnels and aqueducts to the west side of the Snowy Mountains, into the Murray and Tumut River Systems.

Hydroelectric power stations are incorporated in the scheme; the first began operating in 1955, and the total output now is nearly 3000 megawatts. The system has the flexibility to allow water to be released from reservoirs only when needed during the dry season, or to allow water to be transferred between reservoirs. Each year 2500 million cubic metres of water which was surplus to requirements in the east flows usefully westwards. The capital cost, however, was around £400 million.

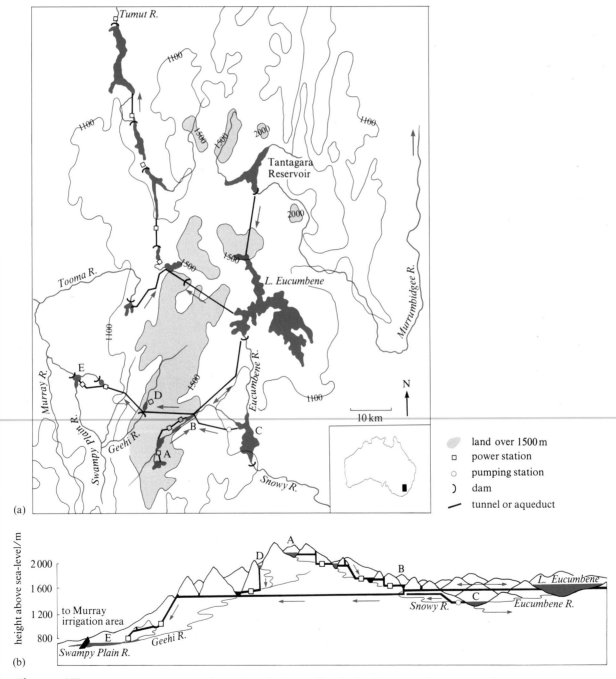

Figure 67 (a) The Snowy Mountains scheme in Australia. (b) A diagrammatic cross-section (not an accurate section). Some of the reservoirs have been lettered A–E so that you can identify the same reservoirs in (a) and (b).

The North American Water and Power Alliance (NAWAPA)

The general idea of NAWAPA was to collect surplus water from the high precipitation areas of the north-western part of the North American continent and distribute it to water-scarce areas of Canada, the United States and northern Mexico. A series of dams and power stations in Alaska and northern British Columbia would collect water and provide power to pump this water up to a reservoir in the Rocky Mountains in south-eastern British Columbia. From the Rocky Mountains reservoir, water would be pumped to another reservoir in Idaho. From there, the water would flow by gravity to the western states. NAWAPA would initially provide 137 500 million cubic metres of water a year to seven provinces of Canada, 33 states in the United States and three northern states of Mexico. The total power generation would be 100 000 megawatts (MW) a year. Out of this, 30 000 MW would be needed for the pumping requirements of the project. The capital cost of the project would be around $100 000 million.

Towing water

Although it is unlikely that any large-scale canal or pipeline water transfer schemes will be developed at present, there is another method of water transfer available to coastal states that is going ahead: transporting water in large plastic bags. There is little capital cost involved, and transport by sea is cheap: the bags can be towed, or transported in the hold of a container ship. The environmental effects are minimal: no land need be drowned.

This scheme is being used at present by water-hungry southern California, to import water from western Canada, and is being considered by Israel, to import water from Turkey.

reaching international agreement to go ahead with the scheme, and there is also an unwillingness to depend on another country for water. The final reason is environmental: both schemes attracted massive opposition on environmental grounds, for drowning land and towns, destruction of wildlife habitats and even the possibility of changing the climate.

7.2 Estuary storage

Estuaries may be used as reservoirs to store water. The water in estuaries is a mixture of fresh river water and seawater. To store fresh water, a barrage can be built across the mouth of the estuary to keep seawater out of the whole estuary, or embankments can be constructed, enclosing smaller river-fed freshwater reservoirs within the estuary.

Estuary storage has many advantages. It avoids flooding large areas of land for reservoirs, and the large lake created in an estuary could also be used for recreation. Cities are often located around estuaries, so water would be available where there is a demand for it. It is sometimes possible to combine an estuary storage scheme with a road or rail link across the estuary, to improve communications in the area. On the other hand, estuary storage also has many disadvantages. The water is stored at the lowest point of the river, at sea level, and it would have to be pumped to all users. River water often contains a high proportion of effluent at river mouths, so the water is usually of poor quality and would require expensive treatment. A barrier would restrict navigation. There may also be ecological problems as estuaries are the feeding grounds of many coastal birds and other animals.

There are two large estuary storage schemes, in Holland and in the Rhine Delta, where water storage is combined with land reclamation, flood protection and communication links across barrages. The Zuyder Zee in Holland used to be a large tidal lagoon, and has been converted into a number of polders (land below sea level) and a large freshwater lake, the Isselmeer. The Rhine Delta scheme involves barrages across the channels in the delta, a combination of flood protection and water storage.

In Britain, proposals were made in the 1960s for barrages to be built across Morecambe Bay to provide more water for the Manchester area, across the Dee estuary for Liverpool, and across the Wash for East Anglia (Figure 68). The original extensive schemes, similar in scale to the Dutch ones, were for a single large barrage in each of these bays. The Morecambe Bay proposal considered several alternative sites for a barrage across the bay, to trap fresh water from the River Leven and River Kent. The scheme would be able to store 328 million cubic metres of fresh water. However, the capital cost was high and the environmental effects significant: the tidal flow to Heysham harbour would be affected, fishing grounds would be destroyed and so would the sea marshes, an important area for wildfowl.

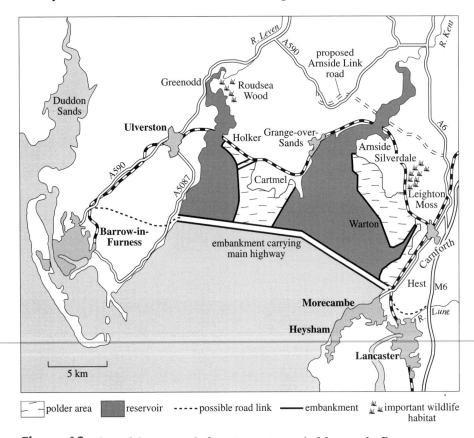

Figure 68 One of the proposals for estuary storage in Morecambe Bay.

The proposal for estuary storage in the Wash involved building embankments to construct reservoirs, which would be filled by pumping from rivers above their tidal limit. These reservoirs would not interfere with the operation of the small river ports in the area, or drown agricultural land or sea marshes.

However, all the proposals for estuary storage in Britain were dropped in the late 1970s because they would be very expensive and inflexible, and it was uncertain whether the future demand for water would make the schemes necessary.

7.3 Conjunctive use

It may be possible to use the water resources of a river and an underlying or nearby aquifer *together*, in a unified way, to provide a better or more flexible water resource than using each separately, by using the storage capacity of the aquifer and the ease of transport of water by the river. This is a **conjunctive use** scheme. The aquifer is used to store surface water when there is an excess of it and it would otherwise be wasted, such as in winter. The river is used to transport water from the aquifer to where it is needed when the river discharge is too low on its own, as often happens in summer.

The storage of excess surface water underground in an aquifer is a type of conjunctive use called **artificial recharge**. This uses an aquifer as an underground storage reservoir. This underground storage has many advantages over surface storage: land is not taken up by reservoirs, there is no evaporation loss, and capital costs are much lower. However, artificial recharge is not a simple process, and it is difficult to do on a useful scale. Surplus water can be introduced into an aquifer either by pumping it into injection wells (this was mentioned in Section 3.4 as a means of controlling saline intrusion near coasts), or by diverting the water into an unlined canal or shallow lagoon in permeable sediments or rock so that the water can percolate downwards into the aquifer (Figure 69). Direct injection of water through wells is more expensive than basin recharge but is used when there is no suitable land for a recharge basin.

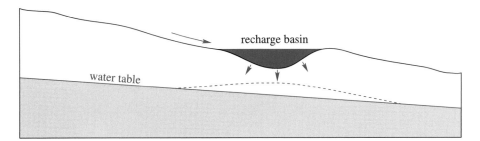

Figure 69 An artificial recharge basin can increase recharge by slowing the overland flow and allowing more time for infiltration. The dashed line is the new water table after artificial recharge.

Storm runoff, which would otherwise be lost to the sea, can be used to recharge aquifers artificially, especially in arid areas. In the Central Valley of California, storm runoff is trapped in alluvial sediments. On Long Island, New York, aquifers are recharged artificially through sands and gravels, which also helps to prevent flooding. In some areas it is possible to use sewage effluent for artificial recharge, as the polluting substances in the water are removed by biological processes during infiltration. However, it is very easy to pollute an aquifer, especially if the effluent contains industrial waste. Another problem of artificial recharge is that fine sediment in the water can quickly clog the pores in an aquifer, reducing the natural rate of recharge from lakes, lagoons and wells.

Artificial recharge is used in the Thames Water area, around London. Here water is often in short supply in summer, and it would be useful to be able to use more groundwater from the underlying Chalk and Basal Sands aquifer. Although groundwater levels in this aquifer are rising (Section 3.7) they are not rising at a sufficient rate to provide the groundwater resource that is needed, so in the 1970s an artificial recharge scheme using injection wells was started in the Lee Valley area to the north of London. The water used for recharge is from the River Thames at times of excess flow. It is treated to drinking water standards before recharge (when spare treatment capacity is available) so that there is no danger of polluting the good-quality groundwater. It is designed to recharge the aquifer artificially over an area of 50 km^2 and provide an extra resource of 100 million litres a day during drought conditions.

Another type of conjunctive use is the use of groundwater to increase the flow of a river, called **river augmentation**. Its advantage is that a river can be used to convey groundwater to its destination without the need to build a pipeline. The effect is similar to river regulation, except that the water is stored underground instead of in surface reservoirs. A disadvantage is that the high-quality groundwater is mixed with river water and will require more extensive treatment before it can be used than would have been required had it travelled through a pipeline.

Groundwater and surface water are closely linked: groundwater maintains the base flow of rivers, and water in rivers can infiltrate into the ground. The abstraction of surface water and groundwater cannot be planned in isolation — one will affect the other. For example, the abstraction of groundwater can reduce the base-flow contribution to rivers by lowering the water table. If carefully planned, however, the conjunctive use of rivers and groundwater can even out the seasonal variations in river flow. In the summer when the river flow is low, water is pumped from the aquifer and put into the river, so that more water can be drawn from the river downstream. The wells must be far enough from the river for the drawdown around them not to make the water table slope away from the river, or water will flow back towards the well from the river (Figure 70). Pumping from wells also intercepts some of the natural base flow to the river.

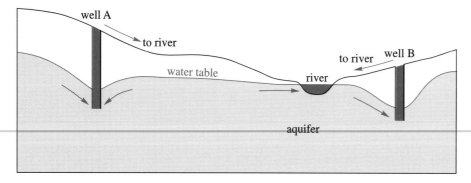

Figure 70 River augmentation using a river and an aquifer. The arrows below the water table show the directions of groundwater flow (in the direction of slope of the water table). Wells must be far enough away from the river (well A) for the level of the water table at the river to be unaffected by the well drawdown. If a well were too close to a river (well B), water could flow from the river to the well, recycling the water put into the river and reducing the net gain. The net gain is also reduced as some of the natural base flow to the river will be intercepted by both wells.

The amount by which natural river flow is augmented by pumping is referred to as the **net gain**, usually expressed as a percentage of the pumped quantity. The net gain is never 100% as some of the additional water in the river always infiltrates back into the aquifer. River augmentation schemes normally show a net gain of water in the river of between 40% and 70% of the water put in from the aquifer.

The Shropshire groundwater scheme

Triassic sandstones are the major aquifer in the Midlands, and are used for much of the water supply (e.g. for Nottingham, Section 6.1.4). The only area with substantial unused reserves in the aquifer is in north Shropshire, in the Severn Basin.

The River Severn is the main component of the water resources strategy in the west Midlands (Figure 71). The river is regulated by water from the Clywedog reservoir in Wales in the summer months, but this is insufficient in dry summers and to supply the forecasted future demand.

A phased scheme of river augmentation from groundwater in the Triassic sandstones in north Shropshire was started in the 1980s with the first two phases completed by 1992 and able to supply up to 100 million litres a day during the summer months, contributing to the 565 million litres a day resource in the River Severn. The net gain is at least 65%. Further phases of the scheme are due to be developed over the next twenty years or so, at a pace consistent with demand. The total yield of the complete scheme is predicted to be 380 million litres a day, at a capital cost of £19.9 million. Not only is this scheme cheaper than building a new reservoir (compare with the size and costs of Carsington reservoir, Sections 6.1.3 and 6.1.5) but it is cheap to operate, is less environmentally destructive, and can be implemented in stages, depending on demand.

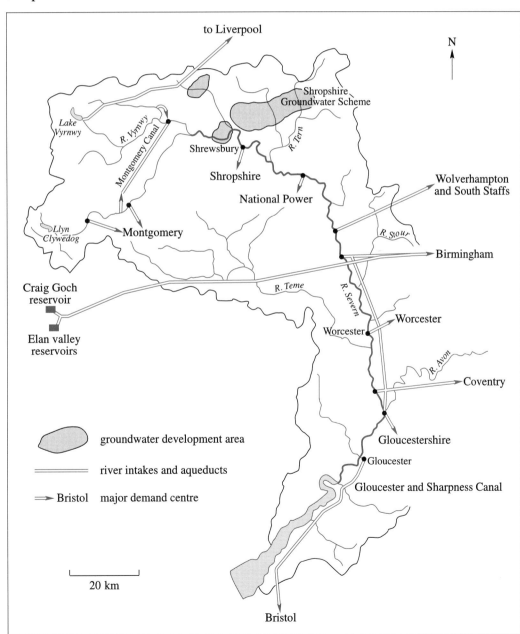

Figure 71 The River Severn water resources and supply system.

7.4 Desalination

The amount of water in the sea is enormous, but before the sea can be used for water resources, dissolved salts in the water must be removed or substantially reduced. **Desalination** of seawater could produce unlimited supplies of fresh water and could solve many water resources problems if it were possible to do it inexpensively. Unfortunately, desalination is an expensive process, producing water costing three to five times as much as that from other sources, as it requires a lot of energy. The other disadvantages are that a large amount of saline water is required, which generally restricts the process to coastal areas (although saline groundwater and water from inland seas can also be used for the raw water), and there is the problem of disposal of the concentrated brine produced.

There are various processes for desalinating water. The one most commonly used is *distillation*, which is similar to the natural evaporation of seawater in the hydrological cycle. Many of the arid countries receive large amounts of solar energy and this can be used as the energy source in a solar distillation process. However, solar distillation needs large areas of solar stills and produces only small quantities of water: a maximum of only 5 litres per day is produced for each square metre of still area. Larger quantities of water can be produced by distillation plants where the saline water is heated by other energy sources, and plants producing over $1000\,m^3$ per day are common. In 1990 there were 7536 large-scale (over $100\,m^3$ per day) desalination plants in existence. Most of the larger plants, such as the one million cubic metres per day plant in Jubail, Saudi Arabia, use the distillation method. Overall, 56% of desalinated water is produced by distillation.

Another important desalination process is *reverse osmosis*. This uses high pressure to force saline water through a semipermeable plastic membrane, which filters out both suspended and dissolved substances. Reverse osmosis is more suitable for desalinating water with a lower salinity than seawater. This method produces 31% of the total desalinated water. The largest reverse osmosis plant at present (1994) is in Yuma, southern Arizona, which treats up to 96 million cubic metres a year of agricultural drainage water with a TDS of $3000\,mg\,l^{-1}$ (seawater is $34\,400\,mg\,l^{-1}$) and is able to reduce this to water with a salinity of $285\,mg\,l^{-1}$.

About 65% of desalination plants are treating seawater and 27% are treating less saline water. The remainder are used for treating effluents or producing pure water for boilers and the electronics industry.

The energy costs are a substantial part of the cost of desalinated water (except for solar stills, which use free solar energy but have high capital costs and low outputs). It takes a considerable quantity of energy to desalinate a cubic metre of water by distillation, around $300\,MJ\,m^{-3}$ for seawater, so the cost of desalination by this means depends directly on the *energy cost*. A desalination plant under construction in 1993 to supply Santa Barbara in California has a capital cost of $36 million for 12 million cubic metres a year, at a selling price of $2.4 per cubic metre.

Desalination is generally only being used where there is no other possible source of water, as all other sources of water would be cheaper, with the possible exception of long-distance water transfer schemes. Desalination is used in wealthy but arid coastal areas, where it is economic to pay a higher price for water. The Arabian Peninsula and Iran, for example, have a greater desalination capacity than all the rest of the world, using energy from their abundant oil resources to produce water; Saudi Arabia has 27% of the global desalination capacity, Kuwait 11% and the United Arab Emirates 10%. The United States has 12%. Other areas where desalination is common include islands with limited amounts of water because of their necessarily limited catchment areas, and where desalination is the only method of increasing these resources. In many cases the desalination plants are only used as back-ups to the normal supply, or to meet seasonal demands. Jersey and the Isles of Scilly, for example, have the only reasonably large-scale desalination plants in Britain, used to meet the summer demand from holiday visitors. The desalination plant on the Isles of Scilly had a capital cost of about £250 000 in 1992 and can produce 220 m^3 per day.

As the technology improves, and the cost of other water resources increases, desalination is likely to become more popular and the cost will reduce slightly. A distillation plant built in combination with a power station, using the waste heat from the power station to drive desalination, has much lower running costs, and these combined plants are likely to become more common. Desalination will probably become increasingly important in the future for the richer arid countries and also as an emergency method of supply in other areas in times of drought, when there is no alternative to the high cost of desalinated water. But for irrigation use, and for the poorer countries, it will be too expensive to use even in times of drought.

Question 35

If the capital cost is repaid over 10 years, what is the capital cost contribution per cubic metre to the selling cost of water from the desalination plants in (a) Santa Barbara, and (b) the Isles of Scilly, ignoring interest charges on the capital? Comment on the difference between the two values.

7.5 Rain-making

Attempting to induce an increase in precipitation by artificial means is called **rain-making**.

The main condition for rain-making is to have water in the atmosphere as clouds; so there is no possibility of rain-making in the cloudless arid areas. For rain to fall, the water vapour in clouds must condense around small particles of solid material, until it forms drops heavy enough to fall as rain (Section 2.2). If there are no solid particles to act as nuclei for condensation, there will be no rainfall. Air without these nuclei may become supersaturated (overladen with water). In these conditions it may be possible to supply nuclei around which condensation can begin, a technique known as 'cloud-seeding'. This will only work for clouds where the water content is high enough for the air to be supersaturated — and the warmer the air, the more water vapour it can contain before the conditions for precipitation are reached. Clouds are seeded with small particles of a substance that has a crystalline structure similar to that of ice, usually silver iodide. Common salt and dry ice (solid carbon dioxide) have also been used. The substance is released into the cloud from aircraft or rockets.

Long-term experiments have been made on cloud-seeding in Australia. In the area of the Snowy Mountains hydroelectric scheme (Section 7.1), where there is relatively high rainfall, the rainfall was increased by about 30% over a three-year period. However, over drier country further west in South Australia, cloud-seeding seemed to have no effect on the low rainfall. An analysis of the cloud-seeding experiments in Australia over 27 years came to the conclusions that it had *no effect* on rainfall in the long term: any short-term increases accompanying cloud-seeding were part of the natural variability of rainfall. So rain-making appears to be no solution to the problems of arid and semi-arid climates.

○ What problems could be caused by interfering with the natural water cycle by rain-making?

◐ The major problem is that artificially removing water from the atmosphere in one area may reduce the precipitation elsewhere; rain-making may simply redistribute the precipitation. Also, if the cloud is moving, the water may not be precipitated at the intended place.

7.6 Icebergs

A large proportion of the Earth's fresh water is in the polar icecaps (Section 2.1), but so far this has not been used for water resources. Ice is formed in both the polar regions, but 90% of it is in Antarctica and most of the rest is in the Greenland icecap. The equivalent of $2000 \, km^3$ of water precipitates onto Antarctica each year, an enormous potential source of water. The problem with using these frozen assets is that the ice is in the wrong place. To be of use as a water resource, it would have to be transported large distances to lower-latitude water-deficient areas such as western South America and Australia, or even across the Equator from the Antarctic to southern California or the Middle East. The most convenient ice to transport would be floating icebergs, which are pieces that have broken off from the main icecaps.

Antarctic icebergs are flat slabs 200–250 m thick and a kilometre long on average, which have broken off from the floating ice shelves that surround the Antarctic land area. Greenland icebergs form by breaking off from valley glaciers where these glaciers border the sea; they have a wide range of sizes, but are generally smaller than the Antarctic icebergs and more irregular in shape. Icebergs float with most of the berg beneath the sea surface, which gives them a draught much greater than that of ships and prevents them travelling in shallow water.

It is technically possible to tow icebergs; offshore oil rig operators have moved them short distances when there has been the possibility of collision with oil rigs. Icebergs have to be towed very slowly, at speeds of less than $2 \, m \, s^{-1}$ relative to the seawater, to reduce the drag. These speeds are comparable to the speeds of ocean currents, so icebergs cannot be towed against currents. The routes of the icebergs would therefore have to be planned to make use of favourable currents, such as the north-travelling Humboldt Current up the western coast of South America. It has been estimated that it would take 3 months for an Antarctic iceberg to reach Australia, and 10 months to reach Saudi Arabia. The melting of an iceberg depends on the temperatures of the sea and the atmosphere, the towing time, and whether there is any insulation around the iceberg. About half of an Antarctic iceberg would melt before reaching Australia.

The cost of water from icebergs is difficult to estimate, because of uncertainties about the energy required for towing and the rate of melting; so far (1994) icebergs have not been used as a water source. Iceberg water will probably never be cheap, but it could prove to be less expensive than water from desalination or from long-distance water transfer.

7.7 Conservation

An alternative approach to extending water resources is by water conservation. One way of doing this is by using less water, by greater *efficiency*, or *recycling*. In countries where water is available at the turn of a tap, water is wasted in houses in many ways — by water-inefficient appliances and unaware people. Industry may also still use water inefficiently, and so does most irrigation, where water is transported to fields through unlined, uncovered canals, and used in surface furrow irrigation. Using water more efficiently, or using recycled water where appropriate, would extend the available water resource.

Another method of water conservation is *substitution*: using alternatives instead of water. On a global scale this will make little difference, as most water (69%; Section 1.1) is used for agriculture, mainly for irrigation, which is a non-substitutable use. However, on a local scale, particularly for many industrial purposes, substitution is possible. Unfortunately, alternatives to water, such as air-cooling instead of water-cooling, are often more expensive and/or less efficient.

The last, and most fundamental, conservation technique is *changing practice*: to change from a water-consuming practice to one that uses less or no water. On a small scale, for example, homes in areas of low rainfall could use only desert plants in their gardens, requiring no watering. On a larger scale, Jordan may need to change its economy away from water-consuming irrigated agriculture (Section 6.2.4). A change for industrialized countries in their consumption of food, to a diet including more cereals and vegetables and less meat, may reduce the water used for agriculture, as it requires far more water per kilogram of meat protein produced than it does for cereal or vegetable protein. The need for irrigation water could be reduced by growing crops that need a large amount of water in areas that have sufficient natural rainfall.

All the methods in this Section are possible, but the extent to which they are used depends on the price of water (raising the selling price will lead to more efficiency in water use, more recycling, more substitution and changing practice) and on our determination, or not, to change our lifestyles to achieve sustainability of water resources. Will it happen? Would you, for example, be willing to give up your dishwasher or lawn, install a water butt, pay more for many manufactured products or eat less meat?

7.8 Summary of Section 7

1   To supplement the water from rivers, lakes, reservoirs and aquifers, the demand for water could be met by water transfer, estuary storage, conjunctive use, desalination, rain-making, icebergs and conservation.

2   Water transfer takes water from an area of surplus to an area of deficit. It has the disadvantages that it is very expensive to transport water large distances and that it causes environmental side-effects.

3   Storing water in an estuary makes it possible to use water that would otherwise be lost to the sea. It avoids flooding large areas of land for reservoirs, and the water is available where there is a demand for it. The disadvantages are that water has to be pumped up to land, the quality will be poor, navigation may be restricted and there may be ecological problems.

4   Conjunctive use is the combined use of a river and an aquifer to provide a better or more flexible water resource. Two types of conjunctive use are artificial recharge and river augmentation. Artificial recharge is the replenishment of an aquifer in excess of natural infiltration, by storing surface water underground when surface water is abundant. River augmentation is used to increase the flow of a river at times of low discharge. An aquifer and a river can be used directly, but at different times of year.

5   Desalination makes seawater usable for water supplies. The process consumes a lot of energy or requires large tanks occupying a considerable area of land, so it is one of the most expensive ways of producing fresh water.

6   Rain-making is an artificially induced increase in precipitation. It can only be done if there is an excess of water vapour in the atmosphere, in clouds which can be seeded to provide nuclei around which water vapour can condense. There is no evidence that it produces a long-term increase in precipitation.

7   The fresh water in polar icecaps could be utilized by towing icebergs to where the water is needed. The relative cost of this water is unknown at the moment, but it would probably be expensive.

8   Conservation is an alternative approach to extending water resources, either by greater efficiency in using water, or by substitution, or by changing practice.

Question 36

Which two of the schemes mentioned in Section 7 appear to be most suitable for supplying water in Saudi Arabia? State briefly why the other possibilities are less suitable. (Saudi Arabia has a very low rainfall and no perennial rivers.)

8 FUTURE WATER SUPPLY IN THE UK

8.1 Prediction of demand

We saw in Section 6.1.6 that about 25 years elapsed between the recognition that increased water resources would be needed in the east Midlands and completion of the reservoir at Carsington to supply this demand. Other major water supply projects have had similar lead times between the recognition of the need and the completion of the project, which indicates that predictions of the future demand for water are essential and must be made for around 25 years ahead.

Prediction starts by looking at how the demand for water has varied in the past. Figure 72 shows how public water supplies varied between 1961 and 1991 in England and Wales. There was an overall increase in total public water supply during this time, but a sharp decrease was recorded in 1976 during the 1975–76 drought.

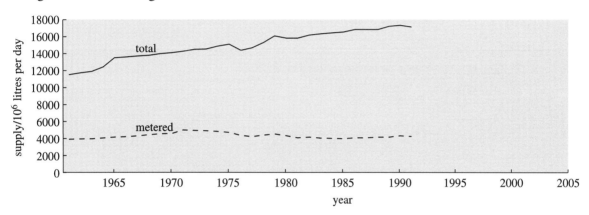

Question 37

What is the percentage increase in the public water supply (a) during the 1960s; (b) during the 1970s; (c) during the 1980s?

Figure 72 The public water supply in England and Wales for 1961–91. (The data come from a different source from that used in Table 2, and are not completely consistent with those data.)

So, although the demand increased between 1961 and 1991, the *rate* of increase reduced during this time. Figure 72 shows that the metered supply varied little during this time, so the demand increased because of an increased consumption of unmetered water. It is mainly homes that use unmetered water; domestic consumption has risen due to overall population growth and the increasing domestic use of water per person. Metered water is supplied mainly to industry: unlike domestic users, industry has a price incentive to use water more efficiently. The metered water demand rose gradually through the 1960s, but decreased slightly after 1973; this was partly the result of an economic recession and partly because changes in the technology of manufacturing processes led to a more efficient use of water. In the 1980s the metered water demand was fairly constant.

Graphs such as Figure 72 have to be projected far into the future because of the long lead times necessary in planning for new water resources. As well as looking at past trends, prediction of the future demand for water involves breaking down the total present demand into domestic, industrial and agricultural components, and identifying the economic, social and population factors which are likely to affect each of them in the future.

Forecasts include assumptions about increases in domestic demand due to greater use of appliances such as automatic washing machines, dishwashers and waste-disposal units, and decreases in domestic demand due to more showers and fewer baths, dual-flush toilets, and water metering to houses. It also includes assumptions about population growth, the level of economic activity, and the rate of leakage from the system.

The assumptions that have to be made to predict demand illustrate the uncertainties inherent in forecasting, and the forecasts may turn out to be highly inaccurate (Table 13). This can be seen easily in retrospect: for example, the 1971 forecast for England and Wales for 1981 was 19 200 million litres per day, whereas the real demand was much less — about 15 900 million litres per day (Figure 72). The 1973 estimate for the year 2000 of 28 000 million litres per day now seems far too high, given the 1991 demand of 17 300 million litres a day: it would imply a percentage increase in the 1990s of 62% whereas that for the 1980s was only 9% (Question 37). For a shorter prediction period the 1987 forecast for 1991 is fairly accurate, but time will tell whether its predictions for 2001 or 2011 are any good. Judging by previous forecasts, they probably will not be. The failure in recent years to make accurate predictions of the future demand for water in the UK has been partly caused by the difficulty in predicting the effects of industrial decline.

Table 13 Forecasts of public water supply for England and Wales

Year of forecast	For year	Demand/10^6 litres per day
1971	1981	19 200
1973	2000	28 000
1987	1991	17 000
	2001	18 250
	2011	19 500
1992	2021	20 500

8.2 Reducing demand

Very few houses in the UK have water meters, so household water charges seldom depend on the amount of water used, and for unmetered houses there is little financial inducement to economize in the use of water. Water, at an average cost to the consumer in England and Wales in 1993 of 53p per cubic metre (0.053p per litre), has always been absurdly cheap compared with other familiar liquids such as milk, petrol or bottled water (all about 50p per litre). If you used tap water at the average rate of 140 litres a day and had a pint of milk a day, the annual cost would be about £27 for your water but £110 for your milk. As well as being cheap, water is also convenient (the only liquid piped to your home) and there is usually no limit on its use. Not all countries use as much water per head as the UK; in countries where the rainfall is less or is seasonal, water will be either more expensive or rationed, and in extreme cases it is available in such limited quantities that the shortage of water is a major factor limiting the economic growth of a country (Section 6.2.1).

People in England and Wales began to be more aware of water supply problems in the 1970s, when Water Authorities began to collect water rates separately from general rates; this made the domestic consumer really aware of the cost of water for the first time. The point that water supplies are not unlimited was made forcibly by the 1975–76 drought, when rationing by standpipes and cutoff periods had to be introduced in parts of the UK.

Drought in Britain 1975–76 and 1988–92

A drought is a lack of rain, or, more precisely, a low rainfall outside the range of values to which society has adjusted. This has happened twice in recent times in Britain, in 1975–76 and 1988–92.

The period May 1975 until August 1976 was the driest period since rainfall records began in 1727 (Figure 73). The preceding winter was slightly wetter than average, but from May to August 1975 the rainfall was only about two-thirds of the average. This continued during the following winter, with rainfall in every month less than the average. Most of this winter rain was absorbed by the moisture-deficient soil, and very little infiltrated to recharge the

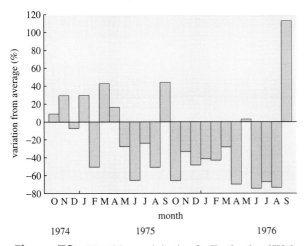

Figure 73 Monthly precipitation for England and Wales October 1974 to September 1976, as a percentage of the variation from the average monthly value. For example, a variation of 0% is the average precipitation, +40% is 40% more precipitation than normal, and −40% is 40% less precipitation than normal.

underlying aquifers (Figure 74). The spring and summer of 1976 continued to have a low rainfall. This was accompanied by very high temperatures from June to August, giving high rates of evapotranspiration, and the soil water zone contained too little moisture for plant growth in many places. Groundwater levels continued to decline and many shallow boreholes became dry. The reduction in base flow also caused a decrease in discharge of many streams and rivers. The drought ended in September (Figure 73), and the following winter was wetter than normal, recharging aquifers (Figure 74) and filling reservoirs. Overall, from May 1975 to August 1976 the precipitation was only 64% of the average.

The second period of drought lasted longer, from November 1988 to February 1992 (Figure 75). It particularly affected southern and eastern England, areas more dependent on groundwater. There were dry spells in the winter of 1988–89, followed by a wet spring, but the summer and autumn of 1989 was also dry. The 1989–90 winter was wet, but the rest of 1990, the summer and autumn of 1991 and up to February 1992 were drier than normal. Groundwater levels were low between the autumn of 1988 and 1992 (Figure 74). From November 1988 to February 1992 the overall precipitation was only 85% of the average for such a period. Infiltration to the Chalk aquifer in eastern England was less than 50% of the average. However, it is worth remembering that because of the very large volume of water stored in aquifers, groundwater is resilient to droughts. The problem is that there are not enough wells to extract the water and those that are available are overpumped in droughts and may fail. The classic examples of aquifer use in droughts are in the Middle East, as in Jordan, discussed in Section 6.2.

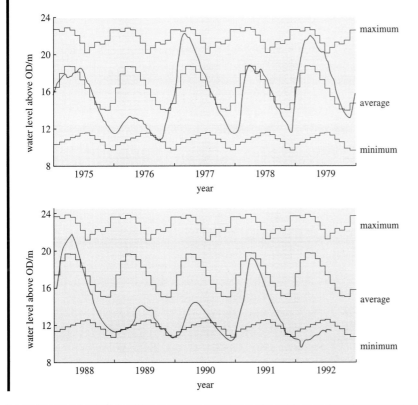

Figure 74 Water levels in a borehole at Dalton Holme in northern England during the 1975–76 and 1988–92 droughts (blue line). The maximum, average and minimum levels are the long-term values.

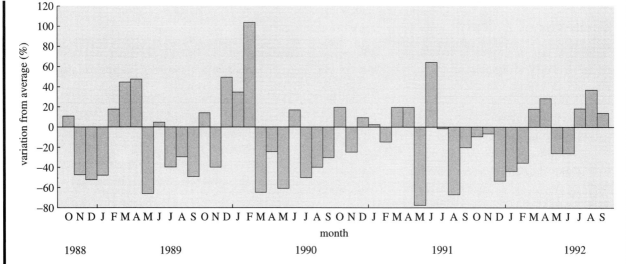

Figure 75 Monthly precipitation in England and Wales October 1988 to September 1992, as a percentage of the variation from the average monthly value.

Many of the economies introduced in the drought had a longer term effect. About one-third of domestic water used goes down the lavatory (Figure 2), and during the drought we were urged to reduce the volume of water used in a flush by putting a brick in the cistern. A dual-flush system, so that the volume of a flush could be altered, would be cheap to fit and could reduce domestic water use by about 10%. Household metering can also reduce consumption, as we saw in Section 1.3. The water supply to industry is usually metered, so there is a financial inducement to use less water, particularly when water charges increase (see Box on 'Water metering').

There is another way of cutting down on the amount of water needed, and that is by reducing the water lost through leaks in the distribution system (see Box on 'Leakage').

Water metering in England and Wales

With a water meter, a household, office or industry pays for the water it actually uses instead of by a fixed charge independent of use. Most homes in Europe and North America have water meters but not in Britain, although offices and industry are usually metered. The fixed water charge for homes in England and Wales depends on the old rateable value of the property, but this system has to change by law by the year 2000. So far there is no general decision by the water service companies on how to change it: should meters be installed or should there be a fixed charge based on the Council Tax value?

The advantages of metering is that it is a fairer system (you pay for what you use, as with gas and electricity), and that metering tends to reduce demand (by 10–25%). Also, water use is reduced at times of greatest demand, by not watering gardens in summer. Use of water meters would also encourage manufacturers to make and advertise water-efficient household appliances, such as lavatory cisterns, washing machines

and dishwashers, in the same way that the manufacturers are now concentrating on the energy efficiency of these appliances.

The disadvantages are the cost of metering and a concern about health. Installing meters would cost about £130–£200 per home or £3000–£4000 million across the country — an enormous investment. There is also a concern on health grounds that some households will sacrifice clean clothes or bathing to economize.

However, some metering, at least, is coming. Most water service companies have trial areas of metering, to investigate changing water use and any side-effects. Many new homes are now built with meters installed — a cheaper way of installing meters. Metering has been an option for most households since 1990, although often at a high installation charge. In 1992 Anglian Water became the first company to decide to install meters for all its customers. However, this provoked so much opposition that in 1994 Anglian Water abandoned the proposal.

Leakage

More water is lost through leaks in the public water supply distribution system (water mains) than is put to any one use. Leakage cannot be estimated accurately, but is around 29% of the water put into the supply, around 5300 million litres a day. The leakage rate is greater in cities, where water mains date back to Victorian times, most of which are now dilapidated. Here leakage can reach 40%.

Water is lost through continual leakage, as well as from spectacular temporary bursts caused by vibration, soil compaction, corrosion or excavation when installing gas pipes and electricity and telephone cables. On average, there are 21 mains bursts per year in England and Wales for every 100 km of water mains — and there were 312 803 km of mains in 1992.

Leakage can, and is, being reduced, by replacing or relining old mains, but it is both very expensive (around £50 000 per kilometre to replace) and very disruptive, involving digging up roads and tunnelling under buildings. Because of this, only 1988 km of mains are being replaced and 2306 km relined each year (1992) — around 1% of the total. Leakage reduction is therefore very slow: we saw in Section 6.1.6, for example, that Severn Trent Water aimed to reduce leakage by about 1% in 1993.

As well as being slow, there is also a technical and economic limit for leakage reduction — how low it could practically be cut to — which is about 14%. But even a reduction from 29% to 14% would save a lot of water!

⬤ If the leakage rate could be reduced to 14% in the year 2011, would the water saved be enough to supply the extra demand forecast between 1991 and 2011 (Table 13)?

⬤ Forecast demand in 2011 (Table 13) = $19\,500 \times 10^6$ litres per day. If leakage reduced to 14% from the 1991 value of 29%, this is a leakage reduction of 15%, so

$$\text{water saved in 2011} = 19\,500 \times 10^6 \times \frac{15}{100} \text{ litres per day}$$
$$= 2925 \times 10^6 \text{ litres per day}$$

$$\text{Extra demand} = 2011 \text{ forecast} - 1991 \text{ demand (Section 8.1)}$$
$$= (19\,500 - 17\,300) \times 10^6 \text{ litres per day}$$
$$= 2200 \times 10^6 \text{ litres per day}$$

Therefore, a reduction in leakage rate to 14% could supply the extra demand in 2011.

However, reduction of the leakage rate to 14% by 2011 is probably too optimistic!

Another factor that may influence demand in future, and which was not taken into account in the forecasts in Table 13, is the *enhanced* **greenhouse effect** — global warming caused by increased emissions of some gases to the atmosphere by human activities, especially by our use of fossil fuels. The effect of this on Britain's climate is uncertain at present but it is likely that summers will get longer and hotter (increasing evapotranspiration) and drier, reducing the amount of water available for supply. The enhanced greenhouse effect will be examined in more detail in Block 4 *Energy 1*.

In general, demand in the future could be reduced by a combination of water conservation, metering and leakage reduction.

8.3 Future supply

The UK as a whole has more water than it is ever likely to need but much of the water is in the *wrong places*: areas with the greatest resources are not the areas of highest demand.

Scotland has sufficient water resources for all foreseeable circumstances and did not experience droughts in 1975–76 or 1988–92. An enormous amount of additional water could be made available by reservoir storage in the Highlands. But nowadays there is a trend towards more flexible schemes. In many of these schemes, rivers are regulated by upland reservoirs, and water is extracted from rivers and lochs in the areas of demand in the lowlands; in others, water supply is developed in conjunction with hydroelectric power generation.

Northern Ireland also has sufficient water resources, most of the supply being provided by surface water sources. Much of the existing storage is in small upland reservoirs, although Lough Neagh, with an area of $385\,km^2$, has become a major source of water for Belfast. Recent studies suggest that abstraction from Lough Neagh could be greatly increased to meet future increases in demand. However, the distribution system in Northern Ireland needs to be more flexible: during the 1988–92 drought there was water rationing in parts of the province.

Wales has a considerable amount of water; but much of it is heavily committed to Welsh needs, or to the needs of the north-west and the west Midlands in England, but there is the potential in Wales for more storage of water if necessary.

England has areas with a surplus of water, such as the north-east, and areas of water deficiency, mainly in the south-east, where part of the supply depends on transfer from other areas. We have seen that in England and Wales the total demand for water from the public water supply is increasing: to understand how this demand could continue to be met in the future we need to look at the water supplies in each water service company area (Table 14). The following question will help you become familiar with these regional differences.

Table 14 Water supply in England and Wales in 1990 (in 10^6 litres per day) and the groundwater percentage

Water service company	Public water supply	Total quantity abstracted	Groundwater as a percentage of total
Anglian	1928	2456	43
Dŵr Cymru	2671	11 474	1
Northumbrian	1060	1098	9
North West	1882	2787	16
Severn Trent	2421	5940	20
Southern	1621	2843	50
South West	630	1003	9
Thames	3827	4131	39
Wessex	798	967	51
Yorkshire	1498	2551	13

Question 38

(a) Which company abstracts the greatest total quantity of water?

(b) Which company abstracts the greatest amount of water for public water supply?

(c) Why does Severn Trent Water abstract such a large amount of water that does not go to the public water supply?

(d) Which two companies get the greatest proportion of their public water supply from groundwater, and which company the least?

The *Postcard Geological Map* can be used to amplify the observations in part (d) of this question.

⬤ What are the main rocks in the Dŵr Cymru (Welsh) region, and in the Southern region?

⬤ The Dŵr Cymru region rocks are mainly Cambrian to Carboniferous. These old rocks have been folded and subjected to metamorphism. They are relatively impermeable and make poor aquifers. The rocks in the Southern region are younger — Cretaceous and Tertiary — and are only very gently folded. They are mainly sedimentary Chalk, sands and clays, of which the Chalk and sands make good aquifers.

⬤ Does the *Postcard Geological Map* suggest that the rocks in Scotland and Northern Ireland should be good aquifers?

⬤ The rocks in Scotland and Northern Ireland are mainly older, igneous and metamorphic rocks, which make poor aquifers. Because of this, only about 5% of the water abstracted in Scotland and Northern Ireland is groundwater.

The distribution of the principal aquifers in England and Wales is shown in Figure 76. The three main aquifers are the Cretaceous Chalk (which supplies more than a half of the groundwater in England and Wales, as it underlies large areas of south and east England where the demand is high), Permian

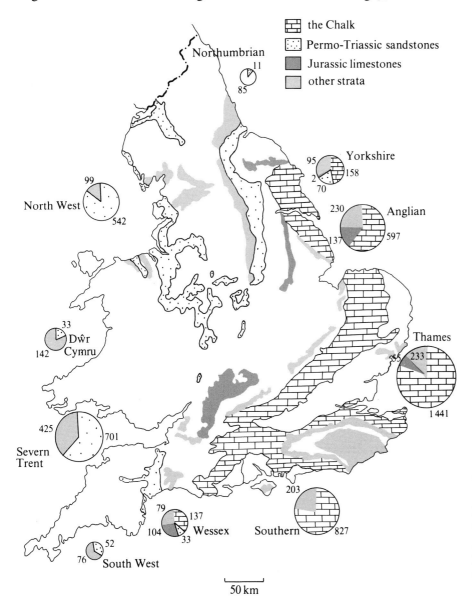

Figure 76 The principal aquifers in England and Wales, and the average daily volumes of groundwater extracted, in 10^6 litres per day, for all purposes in each water service company region. The volume of groundwater extracted is proportional to the area of the circle. Data are for the year 1983.

and Triassic sandstones, and Jurassic limestones. Other aquifers are Carboniferous limestones and sandstones, Permian limestones, Cretaceous sands and Quaternary sands and gravels.

● Using the *Postcard Geological Map*, name the aquifer in the Northumbrian and Yorkshire regions that is shown on Figure 76 as 'other strata'?

○ The *Postcard Geological Map* shows that the aquifer is a Permian sandstone or limestone. However, because it is not shown on Figure 76 as being part of the Permo-Triassic sandstones, it is probably a Permian limestone.

The present regional surplus of water resources over demand in England and Wales is shown in Figure 77. The areas with greatest problems in the 1975–76 and 1988–92 droughts, and most at risk of future shortages, are the Anglian, Southern, Thames and Wessex regions, areas with low surpluses and depending heavily on groundwater supplies (Table 14). If groundwater is not recharged sufficiently in winter, as happened in the winters of 1975–76, 1988–89 and 1991–92 (Figure 74) this leaves insufficient groundwater for extraction during the summer, and also reduces river discharge by a reduction of base flow.

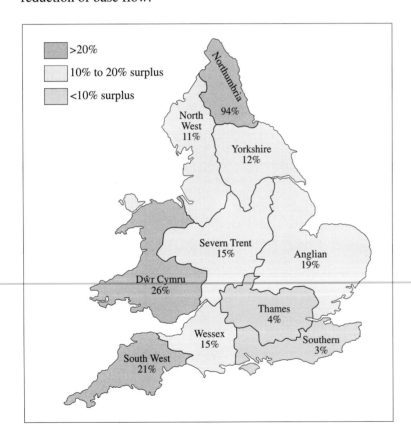

Figure 77 Surplus of water resources as a percentage of the demand for 1990.

However, some areas have more water than they need at present, and at least for the next 20 years or so (Figure 78). The completion of the Kielder reservoir in the Northumbrian region in 1980 doubled the amount of water available to the region, but this water has been almost unused — the demand has only risen by 8% since it was built and the region now has 94% surplus water (Figure 77). Kielder was built to increase the supply to industry in the north-east, such as British Steel and ICI, who expected big increases in demand. Instead, industrial output has declined and their need for water has fallen since 1980. Kielder may be of use in the future for inter-regional

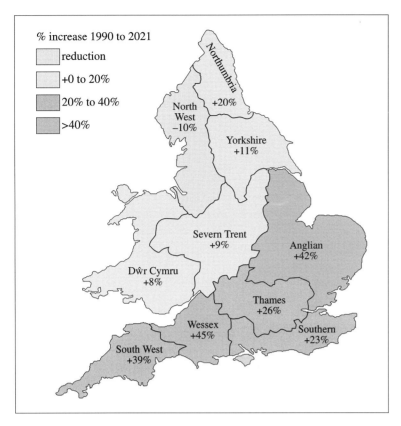

% increase 1990 to 2021

reduction

+0 to 20%

20% to 40%

>40%

Northumbria

North West −10%

+20%

Yorkshire +11%

Severn Trent +9%

Anglian +42%

Dŵr Cymru +8%

Thames +26%

Wessex +45%

Southern +23%

South West +39%

Figure 78 The NRA's projections (1992) of demand for public water supply for 2021. The number on each region is the percentage increase between 1990 and 2021. A negative number for the North West water company area signifies a predicted reduction in demand. The year 2021 was chosen as most large-scale water resources schemes have lead times of about thirty years.

transfers, but at present, as well as being western Europe's largest reservoir, is now possibly its largest white elephant — an enormous boating lake!

There is also plenty of water in the North West region. Here the water demand did not rise during the 1980s, and a fall in demand of −10% is predicted between 1990 and 2021 (Figure 78). Only small increases in demand are predicted for the Yorkshire and Severn Trent regions, producing few problems for supply. The amount of water in the Yorkshire region could be increased significantly by completing the transfer of water from Kielder, which was planned in the 1970s but never went ahead, due to falling demand.

Most of the growth in demand at present, and predicted in the future, is in south and east England, in the Anglian, Southern, South West, Thames and Wessex regions (Figure 78). This is a major problem, as these are also the regions of shortage and are vulnerable to drought. Water shortages in these areas are already causing environmental problems such as reductions in river flow and even drying up of some rivers by the end of summer. Tackling the river problem would mean reducing abstraction — and increasing shortages.

The three most vulnerable water service companies — Anglian, Southern and Thames — want to build more reservoirs to trap the winter and spring flood flows of rivers, which would otherwise flow away to the sea unused. Anglian Water is considering building a reservoir at Great Bradley in Suffolk to store water from Fenland rivers for use in Essex. In the Southern region, a 3.7 km^2 reservoir at Broad Oak, close to the river Stour in Kent is a possibility. Another is the enlargement of the reservoir at Darwell, in Sussex. Thames Water is considering a new 10 km^2 reservoir near Didcot in Oxfordshire to store winter flows from the River Thames, which would increase the supply to Oxfordshire and parts of Wiltshire.

These new reservoirs are large, expensive and inflexible schemes, with long lead times. They would be environmentally destructive, and would be opposed by environmental groups. Are there no alternatives to the flooding of more land?

One alternative, which has been debated many times in the past, is for a national water grid, to transfer water from areas of surplus to areas of shortage. But a national grid in the form of a network of pipelines would be far too expensive, and has never been a practical proposition. However, it would be feasible to transfer water from the wet north and west to the drier south and east using the river system and short aqueducts for transfer between rivers: *inter-regional transfers* (Figure 79). Water from Wales, for example, could be added to the River Severn, and transferred by aqueduct to the River Thames. Also, water from the Kielder reservoir could be transferred south by an aqueduct from the River Tees to the River Swale in order to regulate the River Ouse in Yorkshire, and then water could be transferred water from the Ouse to the River Witham in the Anglian region for transmission to Lincolnshire, Suffolk and Essex (Figure 79).

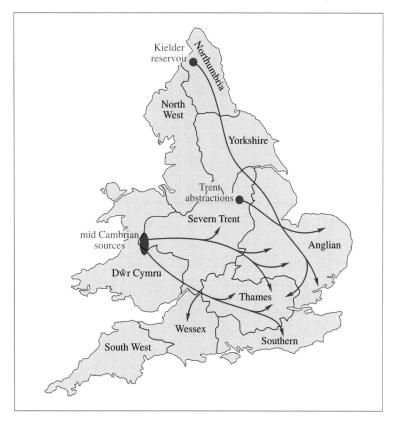

Figure 79 Possible future inter-regional transfers.

On a smaller scale, transfers within a region already exist, and are being developed. Thames Water completed its London ring main in 1993 — an 80 kilometre tunnel about 40 m below the ground surface costing £200 million — to move water around London, between the River Thames and the west London reservoirs and the Lee Valley to the north of London, so that a shortage in one area could be supplied from another area. This will not increase the amount of water available, but does allow it to be used more flexibly.

Another alternative is for greater implementation of conjunctive use schemes, combining the use of aquifers and rivers. These have the advantage of being smaller, have shorter lead times, are more flexible, and have few environmental problems.

The last, 'lateral' approach to water shortages in south-eastern England is to reduce demand — or at least to reduce the rate of increase of demand — by water conservation, metering and leakage reduction. This is an approach favoured by environmental groups.

Table 15 summarizes the options available for increasing water supplies in England and Wales, published by the National Rivers Authority in 1992. The

in terms of unit costs. Bearing in mind the regional resource imbalances, the practical future options are most likely to be:

- demand management (conservation) including leakage control;
- groundwater development, including conjunctive use;
- effluent reuse: either *direct*, where treated effluent is put straight back into the supply (there are no schemes of this type in the UK at present but examples exist overseas), or *indirect*, where effluent is discharged to a river system, aquifer or reservoir and subsequently re-abstracted and treated for water supply (as already occurs widely in some regions of England such as the Thames basin, where treated water effluent is on average 13% of the river abstraction used for public water supply);
- reservoir schemes;
- inter-regional transfer schemes.

Table 15 Options available for increasing water supplies in England and Wales

Option	Indicative cost (£ per litre per day)	Comments
demand management including leakage control	0.1–0.5	some aspects of demand management would lie outside the range of indicative costs
groundwater development		limited potential nationally
direct river abstraction		limited potential
effluent reuse	0.5–2.5	by indirect methods
reservoir schemes		direct supply and regulation
inter-regional transfer schemes		those in the lower range of likely cost
transfers from Europe	2–5	lack of spare resources
inter-regional transfer schemes		those not included in the above category
national grid desalination	4–6	
transfer by ship	much greater than 6	
icebergs/towed water		considered impractical

Source: National Rivers Authority (1992) *Water Resources Development Strategy: a discussion document.*

Activity 10

Consider, if you live in the south or east of England, which option, or combination of options, you would prefer in the future:

(a) water shortages;

(b) more reservoirs (and higher water charges);

(c) water transfer (and even higher water charges);

(d) a change in your lifestyle to reduce your use of water.

If you live outside this area, you might like to consider your reaction, although this will not affect you so directly.

8.4 Summary of Section 8

1 The lead times for water resources projects are quite long (they can be about 25 years) so estimates of the future demand for water must be made for at least this time ahead.

2   Prediction of the future demand for water starts by looking at how demand has varied in the past. The demand for public water supply increased between 1961 and 1991, because of population rise and greater use per person. However, the rate of increase reduced during this time. The unmetered supply, mostly for domestic purposes, increased, whereas the metered supply, mainly for industry, had only a small variation during this period.

3   Prediction of the future demand for water involves breaking the total demand down into domestic, industrial and agricultural components, and identifying the economic, social and population factors which are likely to affect them in the future. However, forecasting remains inaccurate — forecasts of demand for the 1980s made at the beginning of the 1970s were much too high.

4   Domestic consumers in Britain have little direct incentive to economize on water use so far, as the water supply is not usually metered. Substantial economies were made during the 1975–76 drought, and less could be used at other times too. The water supply to industry is metered, so in that sector there is a financial inducement to economize on water use. About a quarter (29%) of the water put into the distribution system in Britain is lost by leakage, but it is very expensive, time consuming and disruptive to remedy. In general, demand in the future could be reduced by a combination of water conservation, metering and leakage reduction.

5   The UK as a whole has more water than it needs, but much of it is in the wrong place. Scotland, Northern Ireland and Wales have sufficient water resources, although part of the water in Wales is diverted for use in England. England has areas of both water surplus and water shortage. Groundwater is a large proportion of the public water supply in the southern and eastern parts of England. It forms only a small proportion in other parts of England and in Wales, Scotland and Northern Ireland, as the rocks in these areas are mainly older sedimentary, igneous or metamorphic rocks, and so are not good aquifers.

6   The area of the UK which will have the greatest problems with water supply in the future is the south and east of England. This area had the greatest problems in the 1975–76 and 1988–92 droughts and is also the area of greatest growth in demand for water. Future increases in water supply in the south and east could come from groundwater development, including conjunctive use, effluent reuse, new reservoirs and water transfer from outside the area. Alternatively, or in addition, demand could be reduced by water conservation, metering and leakage reduction.

Question 39

(a) What percentage of the total water supply in the South West region is groundwater (Table 14)?

(b) The rest of the water in this region is from upland reservoirs (55%) and rivers (36%). What do you consider are the reasons for this distribution between upland reservoirs, rivers and groundwater?

Question 40

(a) During which month of the year is the average groundwater level highest at Dalton Holme (Figure 74)?

(b) Why is it highest in this month?

9 FUTURE GLOBAL WATER RESOURCES

The amount of water used on a global scale has increased rapidly in recent years, and is now increasing by 4–8% per year. The rate of increase in industrialized countries is the lowest, with an expected increase of 2–3% per year during the 1990s. In the UK it will probably be even less. We calculated in Question 37 that the public water supply in England and Wales increased by 9% during the 1980s, which is an increase of about 1% per year. Most of the increase will occur in the developing world, which has a much lower per capita water use at present: for example, an average of 670 litres per person per day in Africa compared with 4630 litres per person per day in North America.

At present, 69% of the global water use is for agriculture, 23% for industry and 8% for domestic purposes (Section 1.1). This division has a considerable regional variation: in Africa, Asia and South America agriculture is even more water-demanding, with Asia, for example using 86% for agriculture. In Europe and North America, industry uses a greater proportion: 41% and 54%, respectively.

Water, however, is a resource in which 'used' is a relative term: some agricultural water and most industrial and domestic water is returned to rivers or groundwater after use, but usually with a change of quality. And we have seen that rivers themselves have a residence time of a few weeks (Section 2.1), so the water in them is renewed on this timescale.

On a global scale, water is not scarce, but locally on a continent or national scale it often is, and with increasing demand is likely to be more so in the future. Twenty-six countries, with a total population of about a quarter of a billion, are already classified as *water scarce*. Many of these countries have high population growth rates and their water problems are increasing rapidly. The water-scarce countries also have another water problem apart from scarcity — the water is often unsafe to drink.

Even in parts of the world where there is little or no scarcity of water, environmental side-effects of water use are often becoming of great concern. This includes not only the obvious pollution, particularly of sewage, nitrates and high salinity, but also the destruction of natural wetland habitats by diversion of water elsewhere, falling water tables due to overextraction, and the drowning of land by enormous reservoirs.

Water shortages could reach crisis proportions in the Middle East and North Africa by the end of the 1990s. Here nearly all the available supplies are already being used. Water management is particularly difficult in these areas where many countries share river basins. Egypt, for example, gets most of its water from the River Nile, whose flow originates mainly from eight upstream countries. In the Middle East, water resources are of strategic concern, and a major cause of war and political conflict. Not all countries are driven to war, but currently (1994) there are major international disputes over water in many parts of the world (Table 16).

Water has been consistently undervalued as a resource. The time will soon come when managing demand through conservation, rather than continuously striving to meet greater demands, will be recognized to be the most environmentally sound solution to what looks like being the first global crisis of the next millennium: water.

Table 16 International water disputes

River	Countries in dispute	Issues
Nile	Egypt, Ethiopia, Sudan	siltation, flooding, water flow/diversion
Euphrates, Tigris	Iraq, Syria, Turkey	reduced water flow, salinization
Jordan, Yarmuk,	Jordan, Syria, Lebanon, Palestine	water flow/diversion
Indus, Sutlei	India, Pakistan	irrigation
Ganges–Brahmaputra	Bangladesh, India	siltation, flooding, water flow
Salween	Myanmar, China	siltation, flooding
Mekong	Cambodia, Laos, Thailand, Vietnam	water flow, flooding
Paraná	Argentina, Brazil	dam, land inundation
Lauca	Bolivia, Chile	dam, salinization
Rio Grande, Colorado	Mexico, United States	salinization, water flow, agrochemical pollution
Rhine	France, Netherlands, Switzerland, Germany	industrial pollution
Maas, Schelde	Belgium, Netherlands	salinization, industrial pollution
Elbe	Czech Republic, Germany	industrial pollution
Szamos	Hungary, Romania	industrial pollution

Sources: Renner, Michael (1989) *National Security: The Economic and Environmental Dimensions,* Worldwatch Paper 89, p. 32, Worldwatch Institute, Washington, DC. Also in World Resources Institute (1992) *World Resources 1992–93*, OUP, Oxford.

Now that you have completed the last Section of this Block, view Video Band 8: *Watering the Desert*, which investigates some of the broader issues of water resources.

Video Band 8   Watering the Desert

Speakers

Rocky Cutis	Yuma, Arizona farmer
Roger Hotchem	US Fish and Wildlife Service
Gary Zahm	US Fish and Wildlife Service
Art Tuma	US Bureau of Reclamation
Joe Skorupa	US Fish and Wildlife Service
Craig Harrison	Water broker
Martin Karpisack	University of Arizona
Dennis Shaftner	US Air Force
Marty Eberhardt	Tucson Botanic Garden
Glen France	Casa del Agua, Tucson
Chris France	Casa del Agua, Tucson
Sandy Smith	The Open University

This programme looks at how water is being used in desert environments in Arizona and California in the south-west USA.

It studies:

1   irrigated agriculture in a desert area;

2   soil salinization;

3   the allocation of water from the Colorado River;

4   the destruction of wetlands by using the land and water for agriculture;

5   the destruction of wildlife by toxic agricultural drainwater;

6   the use and problems of evaporation ponds to dispose of drainwater;

7   the salt balance problems of irrigating a desert;

8   the ability of natural desert vegetation to survive by using little water, using it efficiently and by conserving water;

9   the exploitation of groundwater above its safe yield (mining of groundwater), and the environmental consequences, such as falling water tables and fissuring;

10 efficient water use in a desert, for agriculture by growing appropriate crops, and for domestic purposes.

Two US terms are used in the programme that are not standard British terms:

> *hazing*: this is the scaring of birds from an area by loud noises;
>
> *acre-foot*: a unit used for a quantity of irrigation water — enough to cover an acre of land to a depth of one foot of water, and equivalent to 1.23 million litres.

Fissures in the south-west USA are long cracks that open at the ground surface. They occur in unconsolidated sediment (clay, sand or gravel) that fills deep basins between mountain ranges. Fissures are caused by subsidence, resulting from lowering the water table when groundwater is overexploited. As the pore water is removed, the sediment grains are unsupported, so they compact, leading to subsidence. Different thicknesses of sediment compact by different amounts, producing stress in the overlying sediment, pulling it apart and producing a crack at the surface. Any rainwater that flows through the crack washes away the finer-grained material, thus widening the crack.

The programme demonstrates that the following practices are unsustainable in a desert:

(a) irrigation without drainage;

(b) irrigation without export of salts;

(c) subsidizing irrigated agriculture to produce a crop that can be grown more cheaply, and with less damage to the environment, by rain-fed agriculture elsewhere;

(d) Mining groundwater.

Points (b) and (c) above have also been demonstrated in the Aral Sea region of Central Asia. Ten years or so ago the Aral Sea was the world's fourth largest inland sea, and a very productive fishing site. Then the rivers that drained into the Aral Sea were diverted for irrigation water to grow cotton in the Central Asian desert regions. The sea is drying up and reducing in size, increasing in salinity and killing the fish, ruining the fishing industry. In addition, the irrigated desert is now becoming unproductive because of salinization.

Question 41

(a) How much irrigation water (in acre-feet per year) is needed to grow citrus fruit in southern Arizona?

(b) How can soil salinization be prevented?

OBJECTIVES FOR BLOCK 3

Now that you have completed this Block, you should be able to do the following:

1 Explain in your own words, and use correctly, the terms in the *Glossary* relating to Block 3.

2 Describe and quantify the processes that transfer water between parts of the hydrological cycle, calculate residence times for water in different parts of the hydrosphere, and identify those parts of the cycle that are most suitable for water resources.

3 Recognize the factors that control precipitation, interception, evaporation, transpiration.

4 Using information from wells and the topography of the ground, construct a water table contour map, and carry out the following: interpret cross-sections drawn from it, calculate the thickness of the aeration zone, and the rate of groundwater flow; deduce the direction in which groundwater is flowing; and estimate the depth to the saline interface in a coastal area from the height of the water table and the densities of the fresh and saline water.

5 List the rocks that usually make good aquifers, and estimate how good an aquifer a rock should be, given its porosity and hydraulic conductivity. Distinguish between unconfined and confined aquifers, and recognize conditions in confined aquifers that will produce a flowing artesian well.

6 Using suitable data, calculate the exploitable storage, specific yield and specific retention of an aquifer.

7 Use hydrographs to distinguish surface runoff and throughflow from base flow, and make inferences about the climate of an area.

8 Decide whether a particular site would be suitable for reservoir construction, suggest the most suitable type of dam for a site, and summarize the side-effects of constructing reservoirs.

9 Describe the chemical compositions of natural waters, and explain how and why these compositions vary. Describe the main sources of water pollution, the main types of pollutant and how each type may be controlled.

10 Describe the water resources of (a) the Nottingham district, and (b) Jordan.

11 Describe ways of extending sources of fresh water from the unused parts of the hydrological cycle, or new ways of using existing water sources.

12 Describe how the demand for water in England and Wales has changed between 1961 and 1991, recognize the factors involved in predicting future demand, and discuss the importance of predictions and their limitations.

13 Discuss variations in the amounts of water used in different parts of England and Wales, and how water might be used more economically. Contrast the proportions of surface water and groundwater in the public water supply in different areas in England and Wales, identify the main aquifers, list the possible schemes for increasing water supply in England and Wales, and discuss their suitability.

14 Discuss the future of global water resources.

ANSWERS TO QUESTIONS

Question 1

According to Table 1, a bath uses 80–170 litres of water, and a shower 5–10 litres per minute, so whether the statement is correct or not depends on the length of the shower, the rate it uses water, and the amount of water used in a bath. It would be correct for a short shower (less than 16 minutes for a low-power shower in comparison with a small bath) but not necessarily correct for a longer shower.

Question 2

Average household consumption per person = 140 litres per day

Total household consumption of 50 million people = $140 \times 50 \times 10^6$ litres per day

$= 7000 \times 10^6$ litres per day

Total public water supply (Table 2) = $18\,336 \times 10^6$ litres per day

Domestic consumption as a percentage of the public water supply:

$$= \frac{7000 \times 10^6}{18336 \times 10^6} \times 100$$

$$= 38\%$$

Question 3

Water is only slightly diverted from its normal path in hydroelectric power generation, so this can be regarded as a non-abstractive use. Water used for cooling is diverted to a greater extent and returned at a higher temperature, so this is an abstractive use.

Question 4

The total amount of water abstracted in 1990 (Table 2):

$= 35\,249 \times 10^6$ litres per day

$$\text{Quantity per person per day} = \frac{35249 \times 10^6}{50 \times 10^6} \text{ litres}$$

$$= 705 \text{ litres}$$

This is greater than the average value for industrialized countries, perhaps due to the large quantity of water used in electricity generation.

Question 5

The total annual precipitation over land areas is $111 \times 10^3 \, \text{km}^3$. The total annual evaporation and transpiration from land areas is $71 \times 10^3 \, \text{km}^3$. The excess is $40 \times 10^3 \, \text{km}^3$ annually, which is transferred to the land from the ocean.

Question 6

(a) For Niamey, annual precipitation ranges from about 280 mm (in 1915) to about 940 mm (in 1909). For England and Wales, it is about 790 mm (in 1991) to 1000 mm in (1979).

(b) For Niamey, the minimum annual precipitation as a percentage of the long-term mean:

$$= \frac{280}{562} \times 100$$

$$\approx 50\%$$

For England and Wales, the minimum annual precipitation:

$$= \frac{790}{925} \times 100$$

$$\approx 85\%$$

Question 7

(a) $1\,km^2 = 10^6\,m^2$; $1\,m^3 = 10^3$ litres; $1\,mm = 10^{-3}\,m$.

In England, the volume of water precipitated:

$$= 130\,470 \times 10^6 \times 837 \times 10^{-3}\,m^3$$

$$= 109 \times 10^9\,m^3$$

In Wales, the volume of water precipitated:

$$= 20\,760 \times 10^6 \times 1385 \times 10^{-3}\,m^3$$

$$= 29 \times 10^9\,m^3$$

Therefore, total precipitated $= (109 + 29) \times 10^9\,m^3$
$$= 138 \times 10^9\,m^3$$
$$\text{or } 1.38 \times 10^{14} \text{ litres}$$

(b) The total amount of fresh water abstracted per day in 1990 was 35 249 million litres (Table 2).

Annual amount $= 35\,249 \times 10^6 \times 365$ litres
$$= 1.29 \times 10^{13} \text{ litres}$$

Thus the percentage of precipitation abstracted:

$$= \frac{1.29 \times 10^{13}}{1.38 \times 10^{14}} \times 100$$

$$= 9\%$$

Question 8

(a) June evaporation is almost 120 mm, and that in December is about 12 mm, so evaporation is about 10 times greater in June than in December.

(b) No, precipitation is more evenly distributed throughout the year (Figures 6b and 7), with the highest precipitation less than double that of the lowest.

Question 9

Underground water has the greatest range of residence times, from a few weeks to 10 000 years (Table 3). This is because the shallow underground water moves quite quickly, but the deeper underground water moves only very slowly.

Question 10

The southern hemisphere has more ocean than the northern hemisphere, and as evaporation is greatest from open water, evaporation is greater in the southern hemisphere.

Question 11

(a) Dense vegetation reduces the *rate* of overland flow and thus increases infiltration, although the effect will be offset to some extent by interception, which reduces the *amount* of water reaching the ground.

(b) Water rapidly runs off steeply sloping land surfaces, so there is little time for significant infiltration to occur.

(c) The overland flow is faster on bare soil than on land where crops are growing, so infiltration is less. However, more water reaches the ground as there are no crops to intercept the rain.

(d) Tarmac, concrete and roofing surfaces are relatively impermeable, so that roads and buildings promote overland flow and reduce infiltration.

(e) Frozen subsoil is relatively impermeable and will reduce infiltration.

Question 12

(a) The water table is nearer to the surface of the ground in the northern part, where it is less than 10 m below the surface in many places.

(b) The water table slopes downwards towards the north-east (Figure 17a).

(c) Undulations in the water table follow undulations in the topography. The two major topographic features are the Ryton and Poulter river valleys, beneath which there are corresponding valleys in the water table. A less distinct valley underlies the River Idle.

(d) On the highest ground the water table is about 50 m below the surface. This distance is derived by subtracting the height of the water table above sea level (40 m) from the height of the land surface (91 m).

Question 13

(a) Examples (a) and (c) have grains of fairly uniform size, whereas (b) and (d) have a wide range of grain sizes.

(b) Porosity is greater in well-sorted sediments, because the pore spaces are not filled by smaller grains.

(c) Rocks with rounded grains generally have a higher porosity than rocks with angular grains; for instance, example (a) has a higher porosity than example (c).

(d) Example (a), 30–40%; example (b), 10–20%; example (c), 20–30%; example (d), less than 10%.

Question 14

(a) specific yield = porosity − specific retention

$$= (37 - 7)\%$$

$$= 30\%$$

(b) Essentially, all the 'free' water was removed from an area of $8 \times 10^5 \, m^2$ of water-saturated rock to a depth of 5 m; that is, from a volume of $8 \times 10^5 \times 5 \, m^3$. Therefore, using Equation 3.8:

$$\text{volume removed (the exploitable storage)} = 8 \times 10^5 \times 5 \times \frac{30}{100} \, m^3$$

$$= 1.2 \times 10^6 \, m^3$$

(c) Figure 27 suggests that the aquifer consists of fine gravels.

Question 15

The hydraulic conductivity, K, is calculated using Darcy's law:

$$v = K \frac{h}{l}$$

$$K = v \frac{l}{h}$$

where $v = 0.06$ m per day, $l = 900$ km $= 900 \times 10^3$ m, and $h = 2000$ m. Therefore:

$$K = \frac{0.06 \times 900 \times 10^3}{2000}$$

$$= 27 \text{ m per day}$$

Question 16

The porosity will vary with grain size in the following ways:

(a) For unconsolidated sediments, the larger the grain size the lower the porosity (Table 5, Section 3.5.1).

(b) For consolidated sediments, the larger the grain size the higher the porosity.

Question 17

1, F; 2, G; 3, E; 4, D; 5, A; 6, H; 7, B; 8, C; 9, I.

Question 18

(a) The general shape of the hydrograph indicates a temperate maritime regime, with some contribution from melting snow in April. (The river is a British one, the Severn at Bewdley.)

(b) The maximum discharge is $310\,\text{m}^3\,\text{s}^{-1}$. This is almost five times greater than the average.

(c) The high rates of discharge are caused by large rainstorms.

Question 19

Valley (a) would not be a suitable site as there are permeable beds along the sides of the valley and part of the valley floor. The permeable beds dip down the valley, so water flowing from a reservoir into the permeable beds would escape beneath the dam, and might weaken the foundations as well as losing water.

Valley (b) is not a good site, but is better than valley (a). Permeable beds outcrop over less of the valley sides and floor, and water lost from a reservoir into the permeable beds could not flow down the valley underneath the dam and undermine it, as the direction of dip of the beds is up the valley.

Valley (c) could be a suitable site for a reservoir if the dam were built upstream of where the permeable beds outcrop, so that the water is contained only by the impermeable beds.

Valley (d) is not a good site and is rather worse than valley (b), as water would be lost through the permeable beds to either side of the reservoir.

Valley (e) could be a suitable site, because although it is surrounded by permeable rocks, these are sealed underneath by impermeable beds, so there would be leakage only until the permeable surface rocks were saturated. However, there is a possibility of landslides here.

On balance, valley (c) would probably be the best site.

Question 20

The hydrograph shows a greater discharge in winter than summer. This is mainly due to the greater evapotranspiration in summer; evapotranspiration is greater than rainfall during the summer months in Britain (Section 2.3). Greater winter discharge is only partly due to greater winter precipitation, as Britain's rainfall is fairly evenly distributed throughout the year (Section 2.2).

Question 21

The base-flow contribution on the hydrograph is the consistent flow that is independent of the rainstorm peaks. In November this is about $85\,m^3\,s^{-1}$, for example, and for June about $15\,m^3\,s^{-1}$.

(a) Base flow percentage is about 60% for the winter months.

(b) Base flow percentage is about 80% for the summer months (when there are fewer rainstorms reaching the river, so the proportion contributed by the base flow is relatively higher).

Question 22

(a) The sudden decrease in oxygen a short distance downstream from the sewage outfall is caused by the oxidation of organic material, as shown by the increase in oxygen demand (BOD) just below the sewage outfall. After this, the water is slowly reoxygenated from the atmosphere and from aquatic plants, as the algal population increases.

(b) Ammonia concentrations increase after sewage enters the river, suggesting that nitrogen-containing compounds are being decomposed by anaerobic bacteria. The values gradually decrease downstream as the ammoniacal compounds are oxidized, giving an increase in nitrate (NO_3) concentrations.

(c) Tubificidae and *Chironomus* (both are types of worms), bacteria, protozoa and sewage fungus appear to be most able to tolerate the pollution. These organisms are most abundant in the polluted parts of the river. Anaerobic bacteria are tolerant of pollution.

(d) Those organisms that are able to tolerate the lowest levels of dissolved oxygen are able to breed and thrive in the parts of the river closest to the sewage outfall. They have little competition and few predators. As the level of dissolved oxygen increases downstream, the less tolerant species are able to exist and may compete with others also able to survive there. As higher levels of dissolved oxygen are restored (that is, the river is self-purified), a more balanced aquatic ecosystem becomes established.

Question 23

(a) The EU standards in Table 8 (Section 5.4) suggest that the water is suitable for a public water supply (but it may have to be treated to reduce any organic pollution in the water — organic constituents are not given in Table 9).

(b) The water is unsuitable for irrigation as the sodium concentration is much greater than the combined calcium and magnesium concentrations.

Question 24

A, D and E. Statements B and C are unrealistic; WHO standards allow small amounts of polluting substances in the water (Table 8), including organic material, but no pathogenic bacteria (Section 5.4). F is incorrect: this is the *maximum* acceptable concentration of fluoride (Table 8).

Question 25

(a) Ammonia concentration in the Trent at Nottingham is about $1.3\,mg\,l^{-1}$, much higher than the EU maximum for drinking water of $0.5\,mg\,l^{-1}$.

(b) The increase in ammonia is probably caused by the discharge of large volumes of sewage effluent into the Trent at Stoke-on-Trent.

(c) (i) The River Tame degrades the quality of the Trent (there is an increase in ammonia), and (ii) the Rivers Dove and Derwent improve the quality of the Trent (the ammonia content decreases).

Question 26

(a) Apart from the peaks, the river has a constant discharge and shows no seasonal variation (cf. the River Severn; Figure 42).

(b) The average daily discharge of water from Ladybower reservoir into the River Derwent is about $1\,m^3\,s^{-1}$ (the peaks are too narrow to have much effect on the average).

(c) The water represented by these peaks must also come from the reservoir. The hydrograph at these points, although compressed, has the shape of the hydrographs caused by rainstorms (a rapid rise and a slower fall; Figure 39b) and depicts water that overflows from the reservoir when it is full.

Question 27

The treatment of the groundwater is very simple — just disinfection to kill any bacteria that may be present. The reservoir water needs more treatment. There are four stages to this, in addition to disinfection: increasing pH, adjusting hardness, flocculation, and filtration. River water may have silt or clay in suspension and may contain sewage effluent, so the river water needs additional stages of treatment: initial screening to remove large debris such as branches or leaves; storage to allow suspended material to settle and bacteria to die out; and a final filtration. This is in addition to the four stages listed for reservoir water.

Question 28

Supply in 1991–92 = 195×10^6 litres per day. Forecast for 2021–22 is about 225×10^6 litres per day. Increase = 30×10^6 litres per day.

$$\text{Percentage increase} = \frac{30 \times 10^6}{195 \times 10^6} \times 100$$

$$\approx 15\%$$

Question 29

The Ashop and Alport Valleys have extensive landslips along the sides of the valleys, so would make unsuitable sites for reservoirs.

Question 30

Area = $9 \times 10^4\,km^2 = 9 \times 10^{10}\,m^2$.

Precipitation = $100\,mm = 0.1\,m$.

The total amount of water that falls on Jordan each year:

$$= 9 \times 10^{10} \times 0.1\,m^3$$

$$= 9000 \text{ million } m^3$$

Question 31

Surface area = $200 \times 500 = 10^5\,m^2$

Potential evapotranspiration = $3000\,mm$ per year

$$= 3\,m \text{ per year}$$

Volume of water evaporated in a year = $3 \times 10^5\,m^3$

Percentage of water lost during a year's storage:

$$= \frac{3 \times 10^5}{2 \times 10^6} \times 100$$

$$= 15\%$$

Question 32

$1 \text{ m}^3 = 10^3$ litres.

880 million cubic metres a year $= 880 \times 10^6 \times 10^3$ litres a year

$$= \frac{880 \times 10^9}{365} \text{ litres a day}$$

$$= 2.4 \times 10^9 \text{ litres a day}$$

For a population of 3.5 million, water use:

$$= \frac{2.4 \times 10^9}{3.5 \times 10^6} \text{ litres per person a day}$$

$$= 686 \text{ litres per person a day}$$

This is very similar to the value for England and Wales (705 litres; see Question 4). However, it is used in different ways: in Jordan most (75%) is used for irrigation.

Question 33

The lava has gas bubbles in it, which makes it porous, but these are generally not interconnected (e.g. Figure 26a), so they seldom provide permeability except at the top of the flow, where they are most numerous. The permeability, mainly secondary, results from the way the lava cracked and broke at the top and bottom as it moved. The centre of a lava flow is relatively impermeable.

Question 34

The average domestic use of water in England is 140 litres per person per day (Section 1.2). The domestic demand in Jordan varies from 81 litres per person per day in the main cities, to 35 litres per person per day in areas with no piped water supply. So the domestic demand for water in Jordan is, at the most, just over a half that in England. In part this may be due to the greater use of washing machines and other water-using appliances in England. But it is also due to the situation in Jordan, where water has never been plentiful: where people are accustomed to using water sparingly, and where there is no piped water supply, less water will be used. It is also reduced by rationing.

Question 35

(a) Santa Barbara — capital cost $36 million, output 12 million cubic metres a year. Over ten years, capital cost repayment = $3.6 million per year, which is $3.6/12 per cubic metre = $0.3 per cubic metre.

(b) Isles of Scilly — capital cost £250 000, output 220 m³ per day. This plant is for seasonal demand, so it may work for about 200 days a year. Therefore, output per year:

$$\approx 220 \times 200 \text{ m}^3$$

$$= 4.4 \times 10^4 \text{ m}^3$$

Capital cost repayment is £25 000 per year:

$$= £25\,000/4.4 \times 10^4 \text{ per cubic metre}$$

$$\approx £0.6 \text{ per cubic metre}$$

The Isles of Scilly plant has a capital cost contribution per cubic metre about $3\frac{1}{2}$ times that of the Santa Barbara plant. This is probably due to the economies of scale for the Santa Barbara plant.

Question 36

The obvious scheme is desalination, because Saudi Arabia has abundant energy resources for this. The other untried but likely source is icebergs. Water transfer, estuary storage, and conjunctive use are inappropriate because there are no rivers. The low rainfall indicates a lack of saturated clouds, so rain-making too is unlikely to be successful.

Question 37

(a) Supply in 1961 was about $11\,500 \times 10^6$ litres per day and that in 1969 was about $14\,000 \times 10^6$ litres per day.

$$\text{Percentage increase} = \frac{14\,000 - 11\,500}{11\,500} \times 100$$

$$\approx 22\%$$

(b) Supply in 1970 was about $14\,000 \times 10^6$ litres per day and that in 1979 was about $16\,000 \times 10^6$ litres per day.

$$\text{Percentage increase} = \frac{16\,000 - 14\,000}{14\,000} \times 100$$

$$\approx 14\%$$

(c) Supply in 1980 was about $15\,900 \times 10^6$ litres per day and that in 1989 was about $17\,400 \times 10^6$ per day.

$$\text{Percentage increase} = \frac{17\,400 - 15\,900}{15\,900} \times 100$$

$$\approx 9\%$$

Question 38

(a) Dŵr Cymru abstracts the greatest total quantity of water.

(b) Thames abstracts the greatest amount of water for public water supply.

(c) The area covered by Severn Trent Water is an industrial region and has no access to seawater, only to brackish water in the Humber and Severn estuaries. It therefore has to use fresh water as cooling water for power stations and industry. This is usually abstracted directly from rivers.

(d) Wessex Water and Southern Water extract the greatest proportion of groundwater, and Dŵr Cymru the least.

Question 39

(a) The percentage of the total water supply in the South West region that is groundwater is 9%.

(b) The proportion of water in this area from upland reservoirs is quite high, and the groundwater proportion quite low. The high proportion of water from upland reservoirs arises from factors such as the relatively high rainfall (Figure 8) and the availability of suitable sites for reservoirs in moorland with mainly older, impermeable rocks (see the *Postcard Geological Map*). The low proportion of groundwater must be related to there being only one main aquifer located in the east of the area (Figure 76). It may also be related to the consideration that this area has sufficient water: if there is enough water to be able to choose which source to use, upland reservoirs will probably be more suitable than groundwater because the reservoirs should supply water at a lower cost (relative costs are discussed in Section 6.1.5).

Question 40

March (followed closely by April). The groundwater level depends on the rate of recharge, which in turn depends on how much water is available for infiltration. The precipitation in England does not vary much throughout the year (Figure 6), but evapotranspiration is greater in summer than in winter, reducing the amount available for infiltration in the summer. Groundwater levels are not a maximum in mid-winter, because the rainfall in autumn and early winter is partly used in replacing moisture in the soil, so less of it infiltrates to the water table. In late winter, interception is less, the soil is saturated and most rainfall infiltrates to the water table, giving a groundwater level maximum height in late winter and early spring.

Question 41

(a) Between 4 and 12 acre-feet per year (i.e. a water depth of 4 to 12 feet or 1.2–3.7 m) of irrigation water is needed to grow citrus fruit in southern Arizona.

(b) Soil salinization can be prevented by laying field drains, and using larger quantities of irrigation water to wash the salts from the soil.

ANSWERS TO ACTIVITIES

Activity 1

Domestic water supply   Most of the domestic uses are non-substitutable, such as drinking, cooking and washing. A major use that could be substitutable, although adding complexity, is the use of soil closets instead of water closets.

Irrigation and other agricultural use   Irrigation is non-substitutable and so are many other agricultural uses such as watering stock. However, the use of water for cleaning — for example, washing out milking sheds — could be substituted by the use of straw, or air or mechanical cleaning.

Industrial manufacturing   This uses water mainly for cleaning, conveying, waste disposal and cooling. Many of these uses may be substitutable by air or mechanical processes.

Cooling   Another liquid, air or gas may be used as substitutes.

Hydroelectric power generation   No substitute (apart from substituting another form of energy).

Transport   River and coastal shipping may be substituted by land transport. Marine shipping could be substituted by air transport.

Recreation   No substitute (for this type of recreation).

Overall the major disadvantage of substituting water is the greater cost of substitutes. Water is often used not because it is the *best* washing agent, conveying agent or coolant but because it is the *cheapest*.

Activity 2

These are my results for the first week in June; yours will be different, but these might be useful to demonstrate how to go about this Activity.

Number of baths in a week	= 1
Number of showers in a week	= 3
Time taken by bath taps to fill 1 litre jug	= 2.2 s
Length of time taps run	= 3 minutes, 10 s = 190 s
Water used per bath	= 190/2.2 litres = 86 litres
Time taken by shower to fill 1 litre jug	= 9 s
Water used per minute of shower	= 60/9 litres ≈ 7 litres
Total length of time for 3 showers	= 37 minutes
Total water use for 3 showers	= 7 × 37 litres = 259 litres
Total bath/shower water use per week	= 86 + 259 litres = 345 litres
Averaged bath/shower water use per day	= 345/7 litres ≈ 49 litres

This is about twice the average of 24 litres per person per day given in Figure 2.

Activity 3

The average rainfall from 1970 to 1987 is about 500 mm, less than the longer-term average of 562 mm, so this would generally provide evidence for a period of lower rainfall since 1970.

However, this 1970–87 average has much variability. From 1971 to 1975 the average was below the longer-term average, between 1976 and 1980 it was above it, and from 1981 to 1987 it was below, so this evidence does not support reports of lower rainfall *throughout* the period since 1970 — in particular, 1976–80 was a wetter period.

There have been drought periods in the past, notably the years 1910–18, and the 1970 onwards drier period does not seem to be particularly drier or longer than these past periods, so there is little evidence for a long-term decrease in rainfall.

Activity 4

As $h_1 = 5$ m, $h_2 = 40 \times 5$ m $= 200$ m. For a drawdown of 1 m, new $h_1 = 4$ m and new $h_2 = 160$ m, and the interface will rise by 40 m in an inverse cone shape (Figure 80).

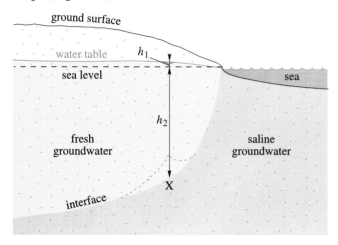

Figure 80 Answer to Activity 4. The dashed lines are the new position of the water table and interfaces between fresh groundwater and saline groundwater on pumping a well.

Activity 5

The groundwater flow lines should be perpendicular to the water-table contours everywhere and the arrows should be in the downslope direction (Figure 81).

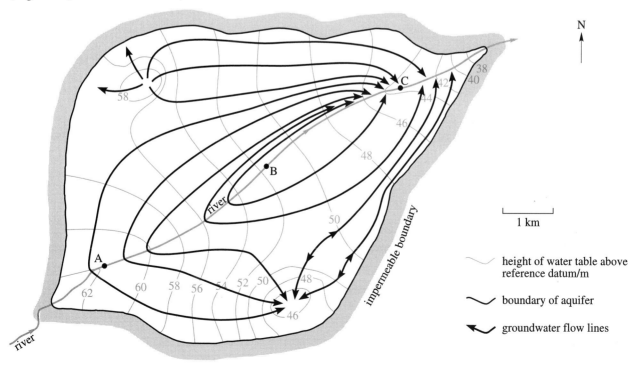

Figure 81 Answer to Activity 5.

Activity 6

(a) See Figure 82. The following is the most likely answer, although alternative interpretations are possible.

Point A   The groundwater flow directions are away from the river, so the water table is probably below the river level, but could be just at the same level.

Point B   There is no groundwater flow to or from the river, so the water table is likely to be at the river level locally on either side of the river although it could also be below.

Point C   Groundwater flows towards the river, so the water table is probably higher than the river (see Figure 137).

(b) When the water table is below the river bed, the river will be dry. Where the river bed intersects the water table, groundwater will provide base flow to the river, so water should appear in the river channel around point B and downriver to the north-east.

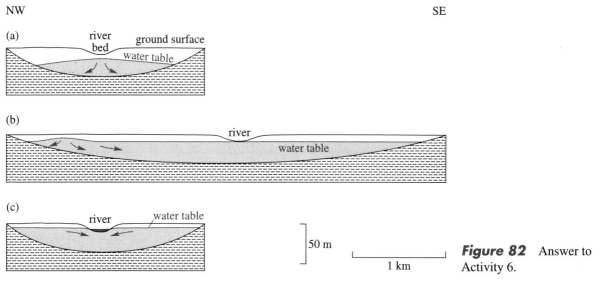

Figure 82   Answer to Activity 6.

Activity 7

Four main sources of pollution are:

1 *Domestic sewage*   This is made up of natural organic materials (mainly carbohydrates, proteins and fats), organic chemicals (e.g. detergents), and living organisms (mainly bacteria); but the main component of sewage is water (99.9%). In some areas domestic waste is discharged into rivers or the sea, where it brings about changes in the chemistry and biology of the water. Domestic waste spread onto land can also cause pollution if washed into rivers or into groundwaters. (You will learn more about this in Section 5.5 on sewage treatment.)

2 *Farms*   There are two main pollutants from farms, both of which can be washed into rivers or groundwaters. The first is animal and plant wastes containing natural organic materials (similar to domestic sewage) and the other is fertilizers, which can be pollutants as they contain the plant nutrients nitrogen and phosphorus compounds. Farms may also be sources of herbicides and pesticides, which are organic chemicals and can be toxic even in very low concentrations.

3 *Industrial waste and cooling water*   Natural organic wastes are produced by food processing industries such as sugar beet factories, slaughterhouses, brewers and canneries. Industry may also produce organic and inorganic chemical wastes: for example, chlorine from paper mills and textile bleaching, acids from chemical manufacture, and chromium, nickel, zinc and copper from electroplating. Water used by industry for washing or

transporting materials, such as in papermaking, will become polluted by sediment in the water; if this is discharged to a river it may make the river turbid, interfering with photosynthesis and animal respiration. Discharges of heated water that has been used for cooling in industry or for electricity generation raise the temperature of river water.

4   *Mining and quarrying*   These provide a source of pollution in the form of sediment suspended in the water (such as washings from china clay pits), dissolved metallic salts, or acidic mine drainage water.

You may have arranged your answer differently and have given other sources or information. What I hope you have firmly in mind is the distinction between the *types* of pollutant and the *sources* of the pollution.

Activity 8

I had two different types of bottled water at home: 'Buxton Carbonated Natural Mineral Water' and 'Mountain Spring Natural Mineral Water, Perthshire'.

(a)   Concentration of dissolved substances/mg l^{-1}

	Buxton	Perthshire
aluminium	0	
bicarbonate	248	128
calcium	55	27
chloride	42	9
iron	0	
magnesium	519	9
nitrate	less than 0.1	1
potassium	1	0.6
sodium	24	6
sulphate	23	6
TDS (of) source	280	128
pH (of) source	7.4	

(b)   The Buxton water has more chloride than the EU guide concentration, but all other substances listed are present at lower concentrations than the guide concentration.

(c)   Bicarbonate is high in both waters. For the Buxton water this may be due to carbon dioxide added to make it fizzy (it is described as 'carbonated'). The Perthshire water is not fizzy and does not mention added carbon dioxide. However, for both waters the TDS at source is less than the sum of the constituent concentrations, indicating that something has been added to both waters.

Activity 9

There is obviously no single answer to this question! It will vary depending on where you live. Below I have given the answers for my house (which is in a small village to the south of Milton Keynes) so you can see the type of answer that could be given.

(a)   Yes, my house has a piped water supply (and life would be very difficult without it).

(b)   I had to telephone my local water company to check on this: although I thought I knew the answer it proved to be more complicated than I expected. I live on a good sandstone aquifer (the Cretaceous Lower Greensand) and expected my water supply to be just groundwater from local boreholes. However, although part of the supply comes from two local boreholes, this water is linked in a water grid to other parts of my water company region, so my local borehole water is blended with that from two major lowland reservoirs, Rutland Water and Grafham Water, 100 km and 60 km away. I presume this is for security of supply and quality purposes.

(c) Again, I had to ask the water company. The borehole water is just filtered and disinfected, but the reservoir water is screened, stored, settled, filtered and disinfected.

(d) In England and Wales you can get this information from your water company on request. I was sent an analysis for my water supply which showed it to be within the EU limits (Table 8, Section 5.4) except for

(i) iron, which had a mean concentration of $0.1 \, \text{mg} \, \text{l}^{-1}$ and a maximum of $0.42 \, \text{mg} \, \text{l}^{-1}$, whereas the EU recommended maximum is $0.3 \, \text{mg} \, \text{l}^{-1}$; and

(ii) ammonia, which had a mean concentration of $0.03 \, \text{mg} \, \text{l}^{-1}$ and a maximum of $0.08 \, \text{mg} \, \text{l}^{-1}$, whereas the EU guide concentration is $0.05 \, \text{mg} \, \text{l}^{-1}$.

The water analysis was for a total of 101 different parameters (many more than in Table 8) and I was also sent the full prescribed concentration list of the Water Act 1989, from which I was able to work out that my supply breached regulations additionally for manganese, nitrite, pesticides and phosphorus.

The water company included details of the non-compliant concentrations under two headings: 'Relaxations', which have been granted by the Secretary of State to 'relax' the standards for naturally occurring substances (the iron and manganese); and 'Undertakings', where the water supply has become non-compliant due to human causes. Both relaxations and undertakings commit the water company to remedial action.

I found the high iron concentration unsurprising, as the sandstone aquifer supplying most of my water has a high concentration of iron. The high ammonia, nitrite, phosphorus and pesticide values are in the reservoir water, and could be caused by agricultural runoff.

(e) I had a water meter installed in 1992, having calculated that it would save money on water bills to my house, and in the hope that it would also provide encouragement for me to use less water (it has).

(f) For 1993 I paid a standing charge of £35.66 for water supply and used a metered $128 \, \text{m}^3$ of water at 53.38p per m^3, which cost $£128 \times 0.5338 = £68.33\text{p}$. So

total water supply cost = £35.66 + £68.33 = £103.99

This is for two people, so cost per person = £51.99.

(g) My house is connected to a sewer.

(h,i) I knew the answer to part of this — that my village has its own small sewage works for primary and secondary treatment — but not the full story. My water company told me that the effluent is discharged to our local small river (the Ouzel) but the sludge is tankered 10 km to the major sewage works in Milton Keynes for further treatment: anaerobic digestion. The digested sludge is then spread on farmland.

(j) The standing charge for sewerage is £34.27 and the quantity charge 73.06p per m^3, taken as 90% of the water supplied (as sewerage is not metered). So

quantity charge = £0.9 × 128 × 0.7306 = £84.17

total sewerage cost = £34.27 + £84.17 = £119.44

cost per person = £59.72

Activity 10

There is obviously no 'right' answer to this activity! Which option you would prefer will depend on your individual circumstances: if your house is about to be drowned by a new reservoir, for example, you may look on option (b) with horror. The points I hoped that you would consider are:

(a) How would you adapt to water shortages; how disruptive would they be; is it worth it for cheaper water?

(b) Are you bothered by more land being flooded for reservoirs?

(c) How much more would you be prepared to pay for your water to get as much of it as you would like?

(d) How far are you prepared to change your lifestyle: a dirty car, fewer baths, no automatic washing machine, replace domestic appliances by low water use ones, no lawn, change your garden plants?

If you feel very strongly about your answer to this Activity, and live in the regions where decisions like this are being made (Anglian, Southern, South West, Thames and Wessex) you might consider what you could do to influence such decisions. Should you write to your water service company, the NRA, your MP, your MEP or join Friends of the Earth or the Council for Protection of Rural England?

Acknowledgements

The author would like to thank the Block Assessor, Richard A. Downing, for his helpful comments and suggestions.

The following student readers are thanked for their comments on an early draft: Julia Adamson, Tom Denne and Iris Rowbotham.

Grateful acknowledgement is made to the following sources for permission to reproduce material in this block.

Figures

Cover: Satellite composite view of Earth, copyright © 1990 Tom Van Sant/ The GeoSphere® Project, Santa Monica, California, with assistance from NOAA, NASA, EYES ON EARTH, technical direction Lloyd Van Warren, source data derived from NOAA/TIROS-N Series Satellites. All rights reserved; *Figure 2:* Water Services Association; *Figure 5a:* ICRISAT, *Climate of Niamey*, Progress Report No. 1, ICRISAT, Sahelian Centre, Niamey; *Figure 7:* Shaw, E. M. (1983) *Hydrology in Practice*, Chapman & Hall, copyright © 1983, Elizabeth M. Shaw; *Figure 8:* Meteorological Office (1978) *Map of Average Annual Rainfall 1941–1970*, © 1978 Crown Copyright, reproduced with the permission of the Controller of Her Majesty's Stationery Office; *Figure 11:* Brandon, T. W. (ed.) (1986) *Groundwater: Occurrence, Development and Protection*, The Institution of Water and Environmental Management; *Figure 12: Water Resources: Planning for the Future*, Anglian Water Authority; *Figure 13:* Reproduced by permission of the Director, British Geological Survey: NERC copyright reserved; *Figure 14:* Peter Skelton; *Figure 15b:* Price, M. (1985) *Introducing Ground Water*, George Allen & Unwin (Publishers) Ltd. © Michael Price 1985; *Figures 17 and 19:* IWEM (1961) *Manual of British Water Engineering Practice*, The Institution of Water and Environmental Management; *Figures 22, 24, 25, 26:* Cargo, D. N. and Mallory, R. F. (1974) *Man and His Geologic Environment*, Addison-Wesley Publishing Company; *Figure 23:* Ward, R. C. (1975) *Principles of Hydrology*, 2nd edn, McGraw-Hill Book Company (UK) Limited. Copyright © 1967, 1975 McGraw-Hill Publishing Company Limited; *Figures 31 and 32:* CIRIA (1989) *CIRIA Special Publication 69*, Construction Industry Research and Information Association; *Figure 34:* Barker, R. D. (1980) 'Applications of geophysics in groundwater investigations', *Water Services*, 84, pp. 489–492, Argus Business Publishers Ltd; *Figure 42:* National Rivers Authority; *Figure 43:* Chorley, Schumn and Sugden (1985) *Geomorphology*, Methuen & Co; *Figure 49:* Sir Alexander Gibbs and Partners, Earley, Reading; *Figure 52:* Hynes, H. B. N. (1960) *The Biology of Polluted Waters*, Liverpool University Press; *Figure 53:* Sir Frederick Warner (1994) *Conference Paper No. 4, Industry and Society*, HRH The Duke of Edinburgh's Study Conference, July 1994; *Figures 54, 59 and 60:* Severn Trent Water Limited; *Figure 55:* Tinker, J. (1971) 'The smug and silver Trent', in Dixon, B. (ed.) *New Scientist*, 50(755), 1971, © IPC Magazines Ltd 1971; *Figure 58:* HMSO (1978) *Surface Water: United Kingdom 1971–73*, Water Data Unit, Department of Environment, © Crown Copyright, reproduced with the permission of the Controller of Her Majesty's Stationery Office; *Figure 62:* Joudeh, O. M. and Taha, M. A. (1978) 'Present and needed information on the water resources in Jordan', *Proceedings of the National Water Symposium*, 19–22 March 1978, Water Authority of Jordan; *Figures 63 and 64:* Willimot, S. G. *et al.* (1963) *The Wadi El Hassa Survey Jordan*; *Figure 65:* Burdon, D. B. (1959) *Handbook of the Geology of Jordan*, Geological Survey of Ireland; *Figure 66:* Bilbeisi, M., *Jordan's*

Water Resources and Their Future Potential, Water Authority of Jordan;
Figure 68: Water Resources Board (1972) *Morecambe Bay Estuary Storage*,
© Crown Copyright, reproduced with the permission of the Controller of Her
Majesty's Stationery Office; *Figure 71:* courtesy National Rivers Authority;
Figures 72 and 75: Turton, P. (ed.) (1992) *Waterfacts 1992*, Water Services
Association; *Figure 74:* Jones, H. (1992) 'The English drought: an impact on
groundwater resources', *NERC News*, Natural Environment Research
Council, October 1992. Data provided by the National Rivers Authority;
Figure 76: WSA (1978) *Water Industry Review 1978*, Water Services
Association; *Figures 77, 78 and 79:* NRA (1992) *Water Resources
Development Strategy: A Discussion Document*, March 1992, National
Rivers Authority.

Tables

Table 4: Pettersen, S. (1958) *Introduction to Meteorology*, 2nd edition,
McGraw-Hill, Inc. Reproduced with the permission of McGraw-Hill, Inc;
Table 15: NRA (1992) *Water Resources Development Strategy: A
Discussion Document*, March 1992, National Rivers Authority; *Table 16:*
Renner, M. (1989) *National Security: The Economic and Environmental
Dimensions*, Worldwatch Paper 89, Worldwatch Institute, Washington, DC.

Physical Resources and Environment

MONTAGUE TERRACE